The Dissertation

POCKET GUIDES TO
SOCIAL WORK RESEARCH METHODS

Series Editor
Tony Tripodi, DSW
Professor Emeritus, Ohio State University

Peter Lyons
Howard J. Doueck

The Dissertation

From Beginning to End

OXFORD
UNIVERSITY PRESS

2010

OXFORD
UNIVERSITY PRESS

Oxford University Press, Inc., publishes works that further
Oxford University's objective of excellence
in research, scholarship, and education.

Oxford   New York
Auckland   Cape Town   Dar es Salaam   Hong Kong   Karachi
Kuala Lumpur   Madrid   Melbourne   Mexico City   Nairobi
New Delhi   Shanghai   Taipei   Toronto

With offices in
Argentina   Austria   Brazil   Chile   Czech Republic   France   Greece
Guatemala   Hungary   Italy   Japan   Poland   Portugal   Singapore
South Korea   Switzerland   Thailand   Turkey   Ukraine   Vietnam

Published by Oxford University Press, Inc.
198 Madison Avenue, New York, New York 10016

www.oup.com

Library of Congress Cataloging-in-Publication Data

Lyons, Peter.
The dissertation : from beginning to end / Peter Lyons, Howard J. Doueck.
    p.   cm. — (Pocket guides to social work research methods)
Includes bibliographical references and index.
ISBN 978-0-19-537391-2
1. Social work education—Study and teaching (Graduate)
2. Doctor of philosophy degree.
3. Dissertations, Academic.   I. Doueck, Howard J.   II. Title.
HV11.L963 2010
808′.066361—dc22
2009022504

1   3   5   7   9   8   6   4   2

Printed in the United States of America
on acid-free paper

For Teresa, Adam, and Matthew; Carolyn, Sarah;
Past, present, future doctoral students

Contents

The Dissertation

1

The Doctoral Degree in Social Work

Being a graduate student is like becoming all of the Seven Dwarves. In the beginning you're Dopey and Bashful. In the middle, you are usually sick (Sneezy), tired (Sleepy), and irritable (Grumpy). But at the end, they call you Doc, and then you're Happy.

Azuma, 1997

THE FEYNMAN PROBLEM-SOLVING ALGORITHM
Write down the problem.
Think very hard.
Write down the solution.

Murray Gell-Mann
(*The New York Times*, 1992)

HISTORY

In 1861, the first three U.S.-based PhDs in any discipline were awarded at Yale University (Walker, Golde, Jones, Bueschel, & Hutchings, 2008);

from this modest beginning, the PhD enterprise in the United States has grown significantly. By the early twentieth century, approximately 500 PhDs were awarded each year; and during that century, some 1.36 million total PhDs were granted (Hoffer et al., 2003). Currently in the United States, it is estimated that about 375,000 people are pursuing doctoral degrees annually (Walker et al., 2008). According to data from the annual Survey of Earned Doctorates, 43,354 research doctorates were granted between July 1, 2004, and June 30, 2005, and 45,596 in the corresponding period for 2005–2006. These degrees were awarded from the 416 universities in the United States and Puerto Rico that awarded at least one research doctorate in those years (Hoffer et al., 2006).

In the field of social work, Columbia University received permission to develop a doctoral program in 1946, and the program's first doctoral degree, a doctorate in social work (DSW), was awarded in 1952 to Alfred J. Kahn (Columbia University, 2008). By 1977 in the United States, there were 35 doctoral programs in social work, 178 social work doctorates awarded, and a total enrollment of 866 students (Wittman, 1979). In the decade of the 1990s, the average number of doctoral graduates in social work was 258 per year (Karger & Stoesz, 2003). By 1999, there were 62 doctoral programs, 267 doctoral degrees awarded, and a total enrollment of 1,953 (Lennon, 2001). In 2005 some 325 social work doctoral degrees were granted to 88 male (27%) and 237 female (73%) candidates and a further 308 PhDs were granted with 80 male (26%) and 228 female (74%) recipients in 2006 (Hoffer et al., 2006). There are currently 81 university members of the Group for the Advancement of Doctoral Education (GADE). This number includes six programs in Canada and one in Israel; thus, there are 75 U.S.-based institutional members that offer a doctoral program in social work (GADE, 2008). The social work doctoral enterprise has also grown significantly.

It is important to note that in the United States, most social work doctoral programs award the PhD degree, although the DSW is still offered by a few schools. Both the PhD and the DSW are usually research-based academic degrees rather than clinical or professional degrees (Thyer, 2002). For the sake of brevity, reference to doctorate or PhD in this book includes these research-based DSW programs, unless otherwise specified.

CAREERS FOR DOCTORAL DEGREE HOLDERS

In all academic disciplines, about half of doctoral graduates pursue academic careers (Walker et al., 2008). However, only about one-quarter of all faculty positions, representing about one-third of full-time positions, are based in research universities (Berger, Kirschstein, & Rowe, 2001). Thus only about one-third of doctoral graduates across all fields can expect to become faculty members at research universities (Gaff, 2002).

For the field of social work there is not a lot of extant information about the annual availability of academic positions. What we do know comes from two relatively recent studies (Anastas, 2006; Zastrow & Bremner, 2004), two older studies (Feld, 1988; Harrison, Sowers-Hoag, & Postley, 1989), and an annual survey conducted by the Council on Social Work Education (CSWE) (see Lennon, 2001, 2002, 2004, 2005). For those readers considering an academic career in social work, the good news from these studies is that there is an oversupply of jobs for graduates with a doctoral degree (Anastas 2006; Feld, 1988; Harrison et al., 1989; Karger, & Stoesz, 2003; Zastrow, & Bremner, 2004).

This oversupply is in part a result of the growth in the number of baccalaureate and master's level programs in social work (Karger & Stoesz, 2003; Lennon, 2004; Zastrow & Bremner, 2004). Of course, doctoral programs do not just prepare students to work in academia, although about half of doctoral students state that they will be seeking academic jobs (Anastas, 2008; Dinerman, Feldman, & Ello, 1999). Results of a survey of 653 social work doctoral students conducted in 2007 revealed that 50% looked to a faculty position as their primary career choice, followed by a research position (14%), administrative (11%), postdoctoral (10%), practitioner (9%), or public policy position (8%), and a further 8% were unsure, with 2% having "other" plans (Anastas, 2008).

A faculty position in a research university may be the goal that many social work doctoral students are encouraged to seek out and would select for themselves, but according to a study of recruitment ads, only about a third of positions advertised in 2005 were in this type of setting (Anastas, 2006). Social work doctoral graduates may thus be in a similar position to doctoral graduates in other fields who face a relative shortage of positions in research universities. In social work, however, this mismatch in "choice" job placements is offset (for the graduates at least) by the greater number of available jobs in any year than there are graduates.

It would appear that the desire to conduct social work research is very significant to aspiring doctoral graduates. Indeed, in terms of their motivation to seek a doctorate, students responding to Anastas's survey cited the following: increase my ability to do research (57%), increase my knowledge in a specific area (47%), change jobs—for example, to start academic career (45%), it was recommended (40%), pursue professional interests in more depth (34%), advance in or improve my current job (28%), earn more money (21%) (Anastas, 2007). The most frequent answer, to increase research abilities, is consonant with the pursuit of a PhD. As you read through this list you may identify some of your own motivations, or indeed you may have other forces driving you that are not contained here. Whatever the case, it may be instructive to examine the attributes thought to be important in potential PhDs and compare them with your own experience and preparation.

According to GADE (Anastas et al., 2003) students accepted into doctoral programs possess the following attributes (or perhaps should possess them): adequate academic preparation, a strong record of academic achievement, motivation, strong intellectual abilities, a commitment to advancing the knowledge base of the profession, and the skills to do so. The skills to advance the knowledge base of the profession are precisely the skills that should be developed and honed by a PhD, but what precisely is a PhD? What does the term imply? What does the work entail? What does the degree confer upon recipients?

THE DOCTORAL DEGREE: WHAT IS IT?

According to Walker and his colleagues, the

> PhD is the monarch of the academic community. It is the very highest accomplishment that can be sought by students. It signals that its recipient is now ready, eligible, indeed obligated, to make the most dramatic shift in roles: from student to teacher, from apprentice to master, from novice or intern to independent scholar and leader. (Walker et al., 2008, p. x)

Although this is a somewhat grandiose description, it is fair to say that the PhD or *Philosphia Doctor* is typically the highest degree offered by universities. In many fields of study the PhD represents the required credential for a faculty position, and even the most cursory perusal of ads for social work faculty reveals this is also true in social work in the United States. (The picture is a little different in parts of Europe with a growing trend toward the professional doctorate; see, for example, Lyons, 2002, 2003; Lyons & Mannion, 2003; Scourfield, 2008).

The significance of doctoral preparation for faculty positions is based upon the rigors and requirements of doctoral education, which "prepares scholars who both understand what is known and discover what is yet unknown" (Walker et al., 2008, p. ix). Walker and his colleagues describe holders of the PhD as "prepared both to know and to do" (p. x). This type of definitional dichotomy arises frequently in descriptions of the PhD and is reflected in many of the concepts associated with the degree, knowing and doing, understanding and discovering, absorbing and creating, innovating and conserving, stewards of the discipline and agents of change. In order to fulfill these seemingly contradictory roles it is important for potential PhD holders to be fully aware of the research methodologies, knowledge base, terrain, and scope of the discipline, and to have the skills to extend all of these by further research. If one thinks of the raw material processed by a university, and thus by faculty members, as knowledge (rather than students), then the relationship to knowledge and its seeming contradictions might be better understood by thinking of the faculty member's tasks as concerned with

- knowledge generation (research)
- knowledge dissemination (publication and presentation)
- knowledge transfer (teaching)
- knowledge application (policy and practice)

The relationship among all of these is captured in Figure 1.1, in which the lower cycle reflects the functional tasks of the academic researcher. The upper cycle represents the task of doctoral students as they move through the process from absorption to generation of knowledge. The "signature pedagogy" of the PhD is apprenticeship (Walker et al., 2008, p. 89), which is ideally suited to the osmotic process by which the student researcher "absorbs" the attributes required to become an independent researcher and engages fully in the knowledge generation, dissemination, transfer, and utilization cycle.

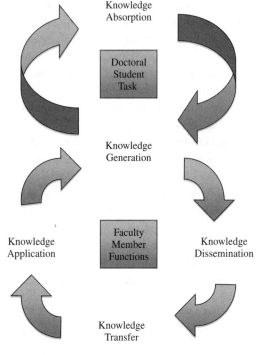

Figure 1.1 Relationship to knowledge

PhD Structure

The structure of a doctoral program might be thought of as a series of hurdles, or as Walker and his colleagues suggest, "a series of milestones . . . coursetaking, comprehensive exams, approval of the dissertation prospectus, the research and writing of the dissertation, and the final oral defense are the most common" (2008, p. x). Alternatively one might think of the PhD as a tripartite venture consisting of the first year, precandidacy, and the dissertation stage (Bowen & Rudenstein, 1992; Council of Graduate Schools, 1990; Lovitz, 2001). Regardless of how it is conceptualized, a PhD most often culminates in a committee-supervised dissertation, which has been defined by GADE as "a student-generated work of independent research and scholarship addressing significant, professionally relevant, theoretically grounded questions or hypotheses" (Anastas et al., 2003).

The dissertation is your opportunity as a doctoral candidate to produce a guided, though substantive, piece of research that hones and demonstrates your research skills. It is both the mechanism and the showpiece by which you make the transition from student of research to research colleague. Although, the dissertation is not a stand-alone research method, drawing as it does from (1) literature review; (2) theory selection, development, and application; (3) research methodology and design; (4) data analysis; and (5) writing, presentation, and defense; it can be conceptualized as a research process unto itself given the developmental nature of the enterprise and the learning process thus engendered.

The doctoral dissertation may be further characterized as the use of a disciplined and methodical process to contribute to a body of knowledge by the discovery of nontrivial information or insights. The purpose of dissertation research is to learn more, not in a vague nonspecific way, but in a disciplined, rigorous, and purposeful way. Completing dissertation research therefore requires discipline, rigor, and purpose. In determining what this means for social work dissertation study, it is helpful to examine the nature of social work itself.

Guidelines developed by GADE (Anastas et al., 2003) suggest there are three interrelated concepts that distinguish social work. First, it is a practical activity, a helping profession. Second, it is a discipline worthy of scientific study. Third, it is a research tradition building a specific body of knowledge. It is the last two of these, social work as discipline and social work as research tradition, that are the focal concerns of doctoral education.

Underrepresented in the formulation above is the central role of values in the profession. This is not unusual. Bisman (2004) has argued that the drive toward knowledge and skill development in social work represents a shifting emphasis in the profession in the balance between knowledge and skills on the one hand and values on the other. The importance of values is echoed in the work of the Carnegie Initiative on the Doctorate, however, with an admonition that PhD programs are not just about intellectual issues and academic preparation but also about a larger set of moral obligations (Walker et al., 2008), further suggesting that PhD holders should "take upon themselves the moral responsibility to protect the integrity of their field and its proper use in the service of humanity" (p. x).

A definition of social work that does encompass social work values and thus reflects this moral component has been posed jointly by the International Federation of Social Workers (IFSW) and the International Association of Schools of Social Work (IASSW) and is quoted in the GADE guidelines:

> The social work profession promotes social change, problem solving in human relationships and the empowerment and liberation of people to enhance well-being. Utilising theories of human behaviour and social systems, social work intervenes at the points where people interact with their environments. Principles of human rights and social justice are fundamental to social work. (Anastas et al., 2003)

VALUES

How do you ensure that your dissertation is striking an appropriate balance between the moral (values) and the instrumental (knowledge and skills)? We suggest that this balance is managed by the manner in which decisions are approached and made throughout the research process. It may be argued that in making any decision the first task is to identify the problem and then to figure out the appropriate objectives to be used in addressing the problem. In contrast, Keeney (1992) argues that the opposite is far better. He suggests that it is preferable to spend a lot of effort understanding central values and objectives and then to look for ways, described as "decision opportunities," to achieve these objectives. This admonition is entirely congruent with social work's strong commitment to values and will help you keep sight of, and enact, important values as you conduct your research.

Notwithstanding the importance of social work values, they are not the only values to be considered. You must also strike a balance between your personal values and the research values of intellectual rigor (e.g., clarity, accuracy, precision, relevance, logic) and intellectual integrity (e.g., honesty, ethics). Figure 1.2 is a Venn diagram representing these three competing value systems. It is our contention that dissertation research is best carried out in the area where all three value systems overlap. In other words, you should strive for the highest degree of congruence among

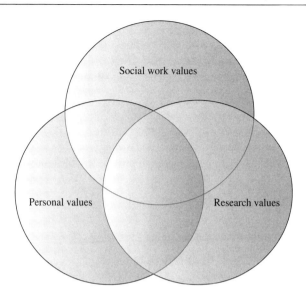

Figure 1.2 Venn diagram: Value congruence

personal, research, and professional values at all phases of the dissertation research. This requirement for value congruence means that you should be clear about the role and influence of competing values when approaching all decisions in the research process.

In the time period when you progress from social work student to doctoral candidate, you will have been thoroughly exposed to and likely will have assimilated the values of the profession. Indeed, you may have been drawn to the profession because of a degree of congruence with your own personal values; this is highly appropriate and to be desired. Difficulties may arise if the commitment to these values, particularly social justice, has an impact that is prejudicial to the completion of rigorous and disciplined research, however.

In the United States, the values of social work are enshrined in the NASW code of ethics: service, social justice, dignity and worth of the person, importance of human relationships, integrity, and competence. Similar codes guide the profession in other countries (e.g., Australian Association of Social Workers [AASW], 1999; Aotearoa New Zealand Association of Social Workers [ANZASW], 2007; British Association of Social Workers [BASW], 2002; International Federation of Social Workers [IFSW], 2004). The value of social justice and its attendant ethical principle admonishing social workers to challenge social injustice and pursue social change (NASW Code of Ethics, 1996, 2008) presents some potential problems to the inexperienced researcher. These problems arise from social work's requirement to pursue social change and the backlash this sometimes brings (e.g., see National Association of Scholars [NAS], 2007). Critics point to real or imagined research design flaws or misguided values that supposedly render research findings or recommendations irrelevant. The possibility that the research really is flawed undermines social work research and the social work profession. It vitiates the profession's historic commitment "to work with forces that make for progress . . . to forward the advance of the . . . common people" (Richmond, 1899, p. 151).

THE SOCIAL WORK DISSERTATION

The juxtaposition of a critical chorus and the possibility of poor quality research is more than a little problematic for the social work profession, particularly because there are some concerns about the quality of social work research (Anastas, 2004; Gambrill, 1999; McMillen et al., 2005), including dissertation research, in which the level of academic rigor is not always as firm as it could or should be (Adams & White, 1994).

Quality

The doctoral dissertation is the capstone of the research apprenticeship for future academic leaders of the profession, and thus the quality of the academic discipline of social work is contingent on the quality of the doctoral research manifested in the dissertation. Notwithstanding the centrality of the dissertation to the profession's research enterprise, Adams and White (1994) examined how public administration dissertation research compared to dissertation research from five other cognate fields, including social work, management, planning, criminology, and women's studies. Though not a perfect representation of the complete dissertation, the authors read 830 dissertation abstracts, including 192 from social work, to determine the quality of the research across seven dimensions. They found the following: (1) Social work ranked last in percentage of dissertations with no explicit theoretical framework or a suggested systematic frame of reference if no theoretical knowledge existed, (2) third in percentage having obvious flaws in the research (e.g., a sample that was too small for the conclusions or generalizing from a single case study), (3) last in percentage with relevance of the research to theory, (4) fifth in percentage of relevance to practice, (5) second in relevance beyond the setting, (6) fourth in percentage of topics that were rated "very important" (though first in topics rated "important"), and (7) last in overall quality ratings of "outstanding," "good," or "adequate." Despite some obvious limitations in the study, and advances in social work research in the intervening period, the findings are troubling.

There are several possible reasons that social work doctoral students might experience some challenges in conceptualizing, conducting, and completing quality research. First, for the most part, much of what constitutes the first years of a PhD program in social work might seem very familiar to a student. Taking courses and studying for exams or writing papers are activities that typical PhD students have accomplished throughout their undergraduate and graduate educations. The process of an independent study or working on a faculty project—with an emphasis on some independence in an apprentice type model—mirrors the typical internship required as an undergraduate or graduate student in professional education, or the role as a clinical supervisor in practice. Once coursework is completed and qualifying exams (or papers) are successfully passed, the PhD experience shifts from the familiar to the unfamiliar. The doctoral candidate is required to design, develop, implement, complete, and report on a fairly large independent research project. This process is unlike any the candidate will have experienced in earlier educational and professional experiences. It is a process that facilitates the development of individuals from students, largely guided by the requirements of a program, their professors, and their committees, to colleagues capable of contributing to the academic literature on their own. Not surprisingly, this is a place where some students can get stuck.

Second, the move from successful clinician/supervisor/administrator to student and ultimately researcher requires several shifts in worldview. Selecting a committee chair and a committee to help guide research can be fraught with anxiety, some real and some imagined perhaps, but the importance of these selections can have profound implications for eventual success as a student as well as the individual's early career (Walker, Ouellette, & Ridde, 2006).

Third, the process of research generally falls into three broad categories: design, measurement, and analysis. Each has its unique issues and challenges and applying the requisite research methodology and statistical skills learned in coursework to an actual project can be especially challenging.

Fourth, social research, agency- or community-based research, behavioral research, research with individuals, or social experimentation as it has been called (see, e.g., Riecken & Boruch, 1974), is a unique endeavor filled with complexities, unique ethical issues, concern for participants, possible political implications (particularly given the social change admonition inherent in social work), and other issues that go well beyond a traditional study. Put simply, "No single scheme has proved adequate to the task of capturing the multidimensional qualities of research strategy and probably none can be devised" (Reid & Smith, 1989, p. 66).

Finally, the process of writing the proposal and ultimately the dissertation has its own set of challenges and complex decisions to resolve. The purpose of this book is to provide you with a framework for analyzing the decisions to be made and a set of tools and techniques that will help you acquire the skills and expertise necessary to propose, design, implement, and write your dissertation.

DECISION ANALYSIS

Decision analysis provides a theoretical framework for understanding the types of decision that must be made in completing a dissertation. It is a prescriptive approach to understanding, analyzing, and improving decision making, which provides a powerful heuristic device. The elements that constitute any decision, according to Clemens (1996), include (1) values and objectives, (2) decisions to make, (3) uncertain events, and (4) consequences.

One of the factors contributing to aspiring PhDs remaining ABD (All but Dissertation) is the lack of clear goal, or losing sight of one's goals. Decision analysis allows for a clear specification of the relationship between values and objectives that helps resolve the "not being able to see the forest for the trees" phenomenon.

In decision analysis an important distinction is made between "fundamental objectives" and "means objectives." This distinction is seen as vitally important. Means objectives are those that are important because they help achieve other objectives, fundamental objectives. Fundamental objectives are important because they reflect what we really want to happen—that is, they are reflective of our values. For example, conducting a literature review (a means objective) may appear to be an important objective, but it is important only because it would contribute to the long-term completion of the dissertation, which represents a fundamental objective; this fundamental objective is worth striving for because it is a decision opportunity allowing the enactment of important values.

Combining the three sets of values (personal, social work, research) at the apex of a sample hierarchy as in Figure 1.3, we can see that fundamental objectives deriving from these values may be to become a "competent social work researcher" and to "complete the PhD." From this higher level in the hierarchy the next level might include "complete dissertation." Below this level the objectives become means objectives—for example, select chair and committee; develop literature review; develop statement of the problem; develop and apply research methodology; collect, analyze, and present data; write dissertation. Each one of these objectives potentially represents multiple decisions, which are addressed in the relevant chapters specified in Figure 1.3. The subordinate means objectives for each of these chapters are represented by the Action Steps contained in the Checklist at the end of each chapter. Completing each task represents one step further in the achievement of the fundamental objectives, which in turn reflect the value set emanating from the three core sources of values.

Conceptualizing completion of the dissertation as a subordinate objective to becoming an effective researcher and completing the PhD is analogous to the manner in which passing the driving test and earning a driver's license is subordinate to being able to drive autonomously. However, it is balancing competing fundamental objectives (complete PhD in timely manner, spend time with family), their subordinate means objectives (complete comprehensive literature review, have it ready for next meeting with supervisor), and their often nonlinear nature (develop statement of the problem prior to literature review and input from committee, revise statement of problem after completion of literature review and input from committee) that constitutes much of the inherent difficulty of dissertation decision making.

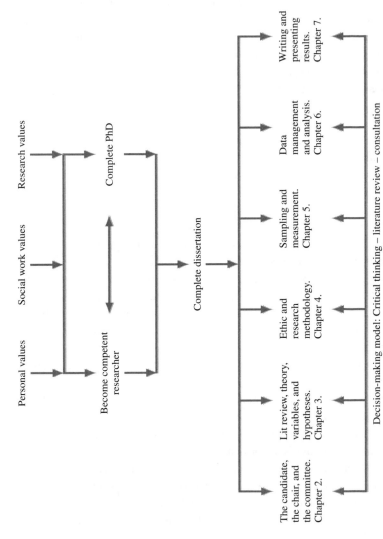

Personal values   Social work values   Research values

Become competent
researcher

Complete PhD

Complete dissertation

The candidate,
the chair, and
the committee.
Chapter 2.

Lit review, theory,
variables, and
hypotheses.
Chapter 3.

Ethic and
research
methodology.
Chapter 4.

Sampling and
measurement.
Chapter 5.

Data
management
and analysis.
Chapter 6.

Writing and
presenting
results.
Chapter 7.

Decision-making model: Critical thinking – literature review – consultation

Figure 1.3 Values, objectives, decisions

Decisions

These sequential decisions, according to the decision analysis model, which occur when a future decision depends upon what happened previously, are referred to as dynamic decision situations. The decision to adopt a qualitative approach as the most appropriate to address your research problem leads to other decisions about the specific qualitative approach (e.g., ethnography or hermeneutics), sample selection, data management and analysis, and so on. The same is true if a quantitative approach is selected; developing a series of research hypotheses is followed by a series of other decisions, each of which is often contingent upon the previous decisions in the sequence (see Fig. 1.3.). Additionally, different information is often available at each decision point, and the decisions may or may not proceed in a linear fashion. In the initial stages of developing your research problem, for example you may begin to conceptualize how you see your research project developing, but your decisions will be shaped and refined as you enter into discussion with your supervisor, and then perhaps again when you receive feedback from your committee.

We propose a model for resolving decisions based on the Feynman Problem-Solving Algorithm presented at the head of this chapter. To this model we would add (see Fig. 1.3) that at every stage in this process you should consult the literature, use your critical thinking faculties, and if necessary consult with your chair and/or committee. The amended Feynman algorithm thus becomes this:

1. Write down the problem
2. Review the literature
3. Think very hard (using critical thinking skills)
4. Consult your chair/committee
5. Write down the solution

Figure 1.3 presents this decision-making framework as showing that decisions to be reached arise from means objectives that can be approached by the use of critical thinking, reference to the literature, and consultation with your committee. We are not suggesting that you invoke your chair and committee for every decision that must be reached or every issue that you must deal with, only for those decisions that you cannot resolve without some input. If you engage in organized thinking, consult the literature, and are still unable to resolve an issue, then you will at least be in a position to articulate clearly what the issue is, and what you require from your chair.

Uncertain Events

Many dynamic decisions in dissertation research have to be made without knowledge of exactly what will happen in the future or what the ultimate outcome of the decision will be. Decision analysis theory stresses that a series of uncertain events that occur between decisions in the sequence compounds the difficulties of decision making. Clarifying what events are unknown and what information is available for each decision in the process is crucial. The capacity to improve decision making is in large measure contingent upon the reduction, to the largest extent possible, of uncertainty. Areas of uncertainty may include information about your own motivation, your skills as a writer, policies and procedures of your department, your specific research question, available resources, committee membership, supervision expectations, and many more. All of these start out with a degree of uncertainty that can be reduced by the use of the critical thinking—literature search—consultation model.

CRITICAL THINKING

One of the qualities that we and others (e.g., Grover, 2007) believe will enhance your experience of the doctoral program is to become an active participant in your own education rather than a passive recipient of the decisions of other people. To function effectively in the role of proactive learner, students require a capacity for critical thinking. In our amendment of Feynman's whimsical problem-solving algorithm, the reference to "think very hard" implies the use of your critical thinking skills.

These skills are fundamental to social work practice in all spheres, including dissertation research, because they are a prerequisite of good decision making. They are also the foundation of ethical and effective practice (Gambrill, 1990; Gibbs & Gambrill, 1999, 2009). Unfortunately, the term *critical thinking* is one of the most common phrases bandied about in education generally and social work education specifically. Almost everybody is in favor of critical thinking, often without applying any critical thinking to their support for or application of it. So ubiquitous has the term become that there is a danger of its becoming meaningless.

What Is Critical Thinking?

The term *critical thinking*, in its current manifestation, has appeared relatively recently. This relatively new origin for the term does not mean that the skills, habits, and behaviors engendered in the concept are also recent. Other names for critical thinking have been used in the past and are still used today—for example, clear thinking, scientific thinking, organized thinking, the critical attitude, critical judgment. Indeed, ever since the Milesian philosophers (e.g., Thales, Anaximander, Anaximenes), there have been attempts to encourage critical habits of thought.

According to Robert Ennis, critical thinking is the "correct assessing of statements" (Ennis, 1962, p. 83). We would not disagree with this definition, provided there was agreement that the assessment of statements also applied to one's own.

Critical thinking has also been defined as

> the process of figuring out what to believe or not about a situation, phenomenon, problem or controversy for which no single definitive answer or solution exists. The term implies a diligent, open-minded search for understanding, rather than for discovery of a necessary conclusion. (Kurfiss, 1988, p. 42)

More simply put, "Critical thinking is the art of analyzing and evaluating thinking with a view to improving it" (Paul & Elder, 2008, p 4.). This latter partial definition encapsulates an important component of critical thinking, *metacognition*—that is, thinking in order to manage one's own thinking.

To achieve some level of definitional consensus, in 1990, the American Philosophical Association published *Critical Thinking: A Statement of Expert Consensus for Purposes of Educational Assessment and Instruction*.

We understand critical thinking to be purposeful, self-regulatory judgment which results in interpretation, analysis, evaluation, and inference, as well as explanation of the evidential, conceptual, methodological, criteriological, or contextual considerations upon which that judgment is based.

The statement further stresses that critical thinking "is essential as a tool of inquiry" (American Philosophical Association, 1990, p. 1). One major underlying theme of all of these definitions is that critical thinking implies organized thinking, which can be reflected in the use of organizing schemata, criteria, or frameworks for the collation, interpretation, evaluation, and presentation of data.

Dimensions

It is clear from the range of definitions above that there is more to critical thinking than merely a formulaic approach to determining the veracity of statements. Gabennesch (2006) describes critical thinking as consisting of three dimensions: worldview, values, and skills. According to Hare (2008), Bertrand Russell's conception of critical thinking "involves reference to a wide range of skills, dispositions and attitudes which together characterize a virtue which has both intellectual and moral aspects, and which serves to prevent the emergence of numerous vices, including dogmatism and prejudice."(p. 12)

Skills

Although there is some disagreement about definitions, there is considerable agreement among experts that critical thinking includes skills in applying, analyzing, and evaluating information. The advent of the Internet has made more information available to more people than has been available at any other time in history. For information to become useful knowledge, however, it must be processed. In terms of critical thinking skills we are referring to the complex cognitive operations required to process information by analysis, synthesis, interpretation, evaluation, generalization, and illustration rather than the more mundane processes of information ingestion and regurgitation.

Traits

One of the central features of the expert consensus described above is that predispositions are as important as actual abilities. Such predispositions as openness, truth-seeking, valuing systematic thought, and intellectual maturity are seen as crucial to the critical thinking enterprise. The consensus statement further describe the habits of the ideal critical thinker, who is

> habitually inquisitive, well-informed, trustful of reason, open-minded, flexible, fairminded in evaluation, honest in facing personal biases, prudent in making judgments, willing to reconsider, clear about issues, orderly in complex matters, diligent in seeking relevant information, reasonable in the selection of criteria, focused in inquiry, and persistent in seeking results which are as precise as the subject and the circumstances of inquiry permit. (American Philosophical Association, 1990, p. 1)

Another important trait requires being critical about our own attempts at criticism. Possession of critical thinking skills is a necessary but not sufficient condition to make one a critical thinker. Practice and application are important to ensure that skills, traits, and habits of mind become manifest as behavior, not just in the analysis of the work of others but of our own.

Specifically, how can these skills, habits, and traits be useful to you in your dissertation? In Chapter 3 we discuss in greater depth the requirements of critical analysis of the literature using Bloom's Taxonomy (1956) and a set of universal intellectual standards espoused by Paul and Elder (1996): clarity, accuracy, precision, relevance, depth, breadth, and logic the adoption of which in the examination of material for inclusion in your literature review, and for the evaluation of your own writing, will help lend cogence and rigor to both. Use of specific criteria for the analysis of the literature is a reflection of, as well as an aid to, critical thinking. Using specific criteria for evaluation in your literature review, for example, might be aided by tabulating the literature, so that the studies under evaluation are represented in the table columns and the specific components to be analyzed and synthesized are represented in the rows (e.g., adequacy of literature review, theory, problem under study, hypotheses, methodology, sample, analysis, results).

The requirements for analyzing and synthesizing ideas and research findings are also manifest as you determine how your research fits into what has gone before and what implications previous research has for your study. In determining how your results fit into what has gone before, especially if they do not accord with previous findings, you will be required to evaluate your own work critically and find the connections with the work of others.

Another crucial role fulfilled by use of critical thinking skills is the evaluation and reevaluation of the boundaries of knowledge in social work research. There is not a finite amount of social work knowledge to "learn" but a continuously expanding sphere of knowledge constantly pushed out by other researchers. The capacity to recognize changes in the intellectual context of the field also requires the use of critical thinking.

OVERVIEW OF THE BOOK

As the foregoing makes clear, this book is not solely about writing the dissertation but is also concerned with processes and decisions involved in conducting successful doctoral-level research. Writing is an important element, but to write about a successful study, one must have completed effective, appropriate, systematic, ethical, rigorous research. This book is therefore intended to be read at any stage in the research process, but it will be particularly useful in the early stages of preparation for a dissertation and as a reference resource throughout. Although not intended as a comprehensive textbook covering all aspects of the research process, this book should provide you with a guide to aid you on your dissertation journey.

In Chapter 2 we examine the three parties in the management of a dissertation: the candidate, the dissertation supervisor or chairperson, and the members of the committee. In addition, we address issues in selecting and working with the dissertation chairperson and committee, as well as the role and tasks of all three parties. The objectives for Chapter 2 include evaluating your own strengths and needs in relation to your dissertation project, the qualities required in the chair and the committee and how they fit with your educational needs, developing a strategy for selecting and working with your chairperson and committee, and how to avoid common mistakes in selecting and working with your committee.

In Chapter 3 we discuss the literature review; the relevance of theory to social work research; strategies and tips for completing a literature search; analyzing, synthesizing, and integrating the literature; developing the statement of the problem; and finally writing the literature review. In addition, we focus on developing hypotheses and defining and operationalizing measurable variables.

In Chapter 4 we describe ethical issues in social research; quantitative, qualitative, and mixed-methods research designs; experimental, explanatory, exploratory, and descriptive research; program evaluation; and the relative merits of disparate models of research, including the requirements of rigor in both quantitative and qualitative studies. By the end of Chapter 4 you should be able to evaluate the fit between research strategies and problems under investigation.

In Chapter 5 we discuss sample size and selection and the measurement properties of instruments; we provide general guidelines for identifying, selecting, and describing a study sample as well as issues to consider when identifying, selecting, and developing appropriate measures. In this chapter, we will also discuss sample selection in quantitative and qualitative research as well as statistical power, effect size, and issues in measurement.

In Chapter 6 we examine issues related to the analysis of quantitative and qualitative data. In addition, we present the application of social research methods and statistics to social problems and social work research. By the end of this chapter you will be able to develop plans for the management and analysis of both quantitative and qualitative data.

In Chapter 7 we discuss strategies to overcome many of the obstacles and issues that make the process of writing seem harder than it should be. By the end of Chapter 7 you will be able to evaluate your writing habits, identify and rectify those that hinder progress on your dissertation, and determine how to organize and present your results

A word of caution: Not everything in this book will suit your circumstances, supervisor, committee, institution, project, or learning style. We espouse the fine social work principle of equifinality; there are many ways to get to the same result, and many ways to satisfy the requirements of dissertation research. We recommend that you engage your critical thinking skills and experience to evaluate the advice provided in this text, and thus determine the most effective strategies for *you* to successfully complete *your* dissertation.

ACTION STEPS CHECKLIST

☐ In relation to your dissertation, make three lists. The first should contain your values, the second those of social work, the third those of the research enterprise. In relation to your area of interest, where do they overlap? Where are they in conflict?

☐ Read previously submitted doctoral dissertations from your institution and from others to gain a sense of the scope, size, shape, structure, and quality required.

2

The Candidate, the Chair, and the Committee

I n Chapter 2 we examine the three parties in the management of a dissertation: the candidate, the dissertation supervisor or chairperson, and the members of the committee. In addition, we address issues in selecting and working with the dissertation chairperson and committee as well as the role and tasks of all three parties.

OBJECTIVES

By the end of this chapter you will be able to

- Articulate your own strengths and needs in relation to your dissertation project.
- Evaluate the qualities required in the chair and the committee and how they fit with your educational needs.
- Define a successful strategy for selecting and working with your chairperson and committee.
- Avoid common mistakes in selecting and working with your committee.

TOPICS

- Dissertation supervision
- Factors that contribute to dissertation completion
- The role of the student
- Mapping your dissertation topic
- Supervisor selection
- The role of the supervisor
- Committee selection
- The role of the committee
- Common mistakes and how to avoid them

CONVENTIONS

In most programs, newly admitted doctoral students are assigned a faculty advisor, often the director of the doctoral program, who remains in the advisory role until a dissertation chairperson is identified. The chairperson may or may not be the original advisor, and the original advisor may or may not be a member of your committee. Throughout this text we use the term *initial faculty advisor* to refer to the faculty person assigned this role. We use the terms *advisor, chairperson, chair,* and *dissertation supervisor* interchangeably to refer to the chair of your doctoral committee.

In deciding which pronouns to use to refer to each party, we have opted for the feminine "she" or "her" to refer to the chairperson, and the masculine "he" or "him" to refer to the student. We have chosen these pronouns somewhat arbitrarily in an effort to be able to differentiate the chair from you—the student, and for the sake of consistency throughout the text. We have also chosen to avoid the somewhat clumsy approach of referring to the chair as "he/she," "he or she," "him/her," or "him or her."

SOCIAL WORK AND DOCTORAL SUPERVISION

If you are like most PhD students in social work, it is very likely that you have had experience (sometimes extensive experience) in a professional social work role before returning to school to pursue your PhD. Indeed,

Table 2.1 Comparison of dissertation and social work supervision models

	Social Work Model	Dissertation Model
Support	Avoiding burnout	Avoiding drop out
Education	Clinical/managerial skills and knowledge	Research skills and knowledge
Administrative	Case/agency related	Dissertation related
Content	Social work/managerial practice	Topic area, research methodology, data analysis
Frequency	Regularly scheduled	Varies by student, supervisor, program
Duration	Specified	Varies by student, supervisor
Prescribed	1 hour for 15 client contact hours for first 2 years	Varies by student, supervisor, program

you may have chosen to continue to work professionally during your program. Seventy-five percent of respondents to a recent survey of social work doctoral students were in some form of employment (Anastas, 2007). Though the survey did not specify, it is likely and we assume that much of this employment was in a professional social work setting. The good news is that social work supervision, whether managerial or clinical, shares some common features with dissertation supervision (see Table 2.1.). First, we will state what they are not. Neither social work supervision nor dissertation supervision is therapy, although they may be therapeutic on occasion. Both types of supervision have administrative, supportive, and educational functions and both should include some form of shared decision making (see Kadushin, 1992; Shulman, 1993). There is also an expectation that both parties, the supervisor and supervisee, arrive prepared for the scheduled meeting, with items for discussion, and work products to review.

If these are some of the similarities, what are the differences? Generally, as a professional social worker, you would expect to meet with your supervisor at fixed regular intervals (Coleman, 2003, p. 2). In contrast, though regularly scheduled meetings for a fixed amount of time may sometimes be the model in dissertation supervision, it is more likely that meetings will be scheduled irregularly at your request or your chair's as a function of your work progress at specified points. Moreover, because both you and your chair have multiple other responsibilities, you may need flexibility with scheduling by setting up appointments far in advance. Such a process may at times leave you feeling frustrated as you seek to move ahead with your study but find your chair unavailable for extended periods. Of course, you might always view such independence as a sign that you are progressing in your work, transitioning from the student role, and gradually becoming a colleague. Be cautious; completing work that is satisfactory to your chair is an essential component of moving forward.

Other differences between job-related supervision and supervision related to your dissertation might arise from the regulated frequency, duration, and amount of supervision in the two models. The NASW Standards for the Practice of Clinical Social Work (2003) recommend at least 1 hour of supervision for every 15 hours of face-to-face client contact during the first 2 years of professional experience. After 2 years, a reduction is permitted to a minimum of 1 hour of supervision for every 30 hours of face-to-face contact (Coleman, 2003, p. 2.). Depending on the needs and wishes of the student, the preferences and availability of the chair, and the policies of the school, doctoral supervision is just as likely to be delivered on an "as needed" or even "catch me if you can" basis. There are differences in function, too; whereas effective social work supervision has the potential to prevent job dissatisfaction and burnout, effective dissertation supervision has the potential to prevent educational fatigue and dropout. Inevitably the educational component looms much larger on the horizon of dissertation supervision. Social work supervision can be seen as a meeting between two professional colleagues with education as one of many functions. Dissertation supervision's primary function is educational, and despite recent recommendations to redefine the concept (Golde, & Walker, 2006), dissertation supervision still operates much like an apprenticeship (Walker et al., 2008).

The most significant difference, however, is likely to be the subject matter under consideration. In the early stages, the content of dissertation supervision may seem intimidating, with familiar topics replaced by the arcane. Discussion of research methodology, for example, may replace discussion of family dysfunction; data analysis may be substituted for the comfort of assessment and treatment planning. The alien subject matter may create a high degree of anxiety-induced dependency ("Hold my hand while I get through this") or may produce a classically conditioned aversion. Some students keen to learn about research methodology may even experience a classically conditioned attraction. It may help if you remind yourself that you are already familiar with some of the components of doctoral supervision. You can use this familiarity as a platform on which to build confidence and eventually competence with the once-unfamiliar content.

WHAT MAKES FOR SUCCESSFUL COMPLETION OF A DISSERTATION?

> Students who create synergy, are proactive in their approach, evaluate opportunities carefully, consider political realities, avoid a deep lull period, manage the interaction with their advisor, seek help and criticism of their work, build a particular skill set, temper ambitious projects with reasoned reality, and don't leave the program prematurely tend to be successful. (Grover, 2007, p. 18)

There you have it. All you need do is follow Grover's advice and you will fly through unscathed. As one of our colleagues is fond of saying, however, "The devil is in the details." These details sometimes lead to delay or even failure to complete the dissertation; just ask any ABD (which in addition to meaning All but Dissertation also stands for All but the Details).

Delayed completion and failure to complete dissertations and theses for research degrees have been enduring problems (Burnett, 1999; Garcia, Malot, & Brethower, 1988; Golde & Walker, 2006; Nettles & Millett, 2006; Rudd, 1985; Thurgood, Golladay, & Hill, 2006; Walker, Ouellette, & Ridd, 2006; Young, Fogarty, & McRea, 1987). In a study in the United Kingdom, Rudd (1985) reported 40% to 50% noncompletion rates for postgraduate students. Factors in supervision have been implicated in high noncompletion rates, especially in the social sciences where dissatisfaction with the quality of supervision have been reported at higher rates than in the natural sciences (Young et al., 1987).

Little research has been conducted on social work doctorates in the United States other than the data and count reported yearly by the

Council on Social Work Education (CSWE) (Lennon, 2004, 2005). Even so, we do know that many students who begin doctoral studies in social work do not complete them, and that there are current and projected shortages of doctoral graduates for faculty positions in social work (Robb, 2005; Zastrow & Bremner, 2004). Anastas recently reported results of a survey of 801 social work doctoral students from programs throughout North America (Anastas, 2007, 2008). Although 93.7% of respondents had an assigned faculty member or research advisor, 14% of total respondents were not satisfied with their dissertation supervision. Almost 73% of the students surveyed reported having one or more mentors in the program, and almost 56% reported having an external mentor. On a 5-point scale, mean satisfaction with mentors was 4.47 and faculty research advisors 3.96.

Though there is a lack of outcome data on social work doctoral programs (Anastas, 2007), the nature and process of supervision has been implicated as a significant contributor to completion problems in these programs (Dillon & Malott, 1981; Erdem & Ozen, 2003; Grover, 2001; Hockey, 1991). Poor direction and structure (Acker, Hill, & Black, 1994), lack of fit with supervisor and student interests, and inadequate guidance and structuring of time (Eggleston & Delamont, 1983; Wright & Lodwick, 1989) have also been shown to contribute to problems in dissertation completion. In a cross-disciplinary study, Seagram and her colleagues (Seagram, Gould, & Pyke, 1998) reported on factors associated with time-to-completion of doctoral programs. A combination of the factors—beginning the dissertation early, sticking with the same topic and supervisor, frequency of supervisory meetings, and collaboration with supervisor on conference presentations—predicted 30% of the variance in time-to-completion. However, the authors point to the number of micro inequities experienced by women in higher education that create a "chilly climate" for women (Seagram et al., 1998). Although they reported no significant difference in time-to-completion by gender, females did express lower levels of satisfaction with the quality of supervisory and committee support. In Anastas's survey of social work doctoral students, some 78% were female, and 61% of those surveyed were assigned a same-sex faculty member.

Clearly the issue of student/supervisor compatibility is of the utmost importance (Schniederjans, 2007). Fields (1998) has suggested that supervision may be the crucial difference between completion and non-completion of a research degree. Despite this importance, Ray (2007) has suggested that

> selecting a supervisor is often done in an unplanned manner, which can become one of the reasons for regret, lack of motivation, and poor quality of research output. The need for having a supervisor who fits well with the students' preferences can hardly be overemphasized. This requires that students should select their supervisor in an objective manner, taking all factors and their own priorities into account. (p. 23)

WHAT SHOULD YOU DO?

Ultimately, your role is to become a competent and effective scholar through the dissertation process, but at this stage your role is to be an informed consumer in selecting a supervisor. While it must be recognized that selection is reciprocal, in that the supervisor must also select you, it is an important decision with the potential for long-term career consequences. We recognize, of course, that for some of you there is limited choice in supervisor selection and for some of you no choice at all. Even so, to have a proactive conversation with your supervisor about completing your dissertation, it remains important that you know both the broad requirements of the supervisory role and your specific needs.

As we saw in Chapter 1, choices are decision opportunities and can be used to maximize the achievement of values and outcomes. Value clarification is a matter of deciding what is important to you. Personal values, the values of intellectual rigor, social work values, and the value of education are of great significance at this stage. Of course, you may value making a meaningful contribution to the field, perhaps starting with a "magnum opus" dissertation. As we have seen, it may be important that you balance such values with the reality of successful and timely completion of your dissertation. Stated simply, educationally you are interested in a chair who can facilitate your developing research knowledge and skills, help focus your attention on the necessary tasks at hand, and facilitate your journey to successful completion.

The appropriate objectives in selecting a chair or supervisor arise from the value of education (somebody from whom you can learn), the value of completion (somebody who can help you navigate the dissertation process), the value of life (somebody who can help you through the dissertation process in one piece, without spending too much of your life in thrall to the dissertation).

It is helpful also to be clear about the role and influence of competing values when approaching all decisions in this process. For example, you may value collegiality and thus may be drawn to a particularly sociable faculty member or one with whom you have a good rapport. This is not necessarily bad, but it is a poor criterion on which to base such a significant decision. It might be pleasant to have a cozy relationship with your supervisor, but such a relationship may sour if you cannot get through to completion, nor is such a relationship a guarantee that the process will be less fraught with difficulties.

Before moving on to the issue of selection of the dissertation chair, there are some important student-related considerations to address. Grover (2007) posits that to be successful in a doctoral program, students must be "effective managers and proactive participants in their evolutionary process" (p. 10). This suggests that you have to take responsibility for a number of actions and choices. In decision analysis terms these choices lead to means objectives: the things that must be done to achieve the fundamental objective for this stage, which is to select a suitable chairperson. The first of these objectives is concerned with assuming responsibility.

One important factor in assuming responsibility is ownership; with ownership comes responsibility. Ask yourself who owns the dissertation. To answer the question of ownership, it is enough to ask whose degree this is. It is yours. Your colleagues, committee members, and chair will not take your classes, present and defend your proposal, carry out your research, write your dissertation, or conduct your defense. You will.

Although we stress that as a student you "own" the dissertation in all its aspects, this does not mean you have supreme power or decision-making autonomy in all aspects of project development and completion. It does mean, however, that you are responsible for ensuring the completion of all necessary tasks.

The dissertation process is a system of mutual obligations and responsibilities. The role of preparing doctoral students involves an obligation on the faculty to meet student needs (Wanta, Parsons, Dunwoody, Barton, & Barnes, 2003), but obligations do not accrue only to faculty. Students also have considerable responsibilities in contributing to the success of the supervisory dyad.

Schniederjans (2007) has developed a basic bill of rights for doctoral students, which he suggests students should affirm with prospective faculty members before making a final decision on chair selection. He also recommends that "prospective committee chairs carefully consider the ramifications of the role when opting to be a committee chair" (p. 7). Table 2.2 presents an adaptation of the basic rights developed by Schniederjans, in which we have changed "obligations of the student" in the original to "rights for the supervisor." You can see from the table that your right to select the most qualified chair is balanced by the chair's right to expect that you are diligent in seeking out a prospective chair. This diligence should not be restricted to research about the chair, however. Due diligence involves making yourself the subject of your research. Before you move on to questions about prospective supervisors there are some things that it would be helpful to articulate about yourself.

How do you respond to feedback? What kind of feedback is most effective for you? What kind of structure do you need? How much autonomy are you comfortable with? Do you care about the level of warmth between you and your chair? All of these are questions to address in terms of needs, and they are mirrored in what you hope to get from your dissertation supervisor.

A useful task in selecting both your chairperson and committee members is to take an inventory of your strengths and needs in relation to the research endeavor you are undertaking. Exhibit 2.1 contains a series of questions to help determine what you have, and thus what you may need. These questions deal with your personal readiness and motivation, topic area, methodology, literature research, data analysis, and writing knowledge and skills. Many of the questions ask about your "working familiarity" with various techniques, but we are not suggesting at the chair selection stage of your dissertation that you should have developed this working familiarity with all of these topics. To pass your competency exams, you will have developed a degree of knowledge and a working familiarity with some of the topics. The intent now is that you identify where you are so you can decide how to get to where you want to be. You should be able to answer yes to all of these questions by the end of your program.

Being an educated consumer implies a diligent search for information to help guide decision making. How one goes about this is in the

Table 2.2 Basic Rights for Doctoral Students and Committee Chairs

Time scale	Students should have the right to . . .	Chairs should have the right to . . .
Initial	Select the most qualified faculty member for the dissertation subject.	Expect that students will conduct diligent research in seeking prospective chairs who have research expertise in the student's proposed topic area.
Ongoing	Expect faculty to meet their obligations to their programs in a timely manner or allow the students to seek replacements.	Expect that students will deal with any personal problems that might impinge upon their role performance in the dissertation process. Expect that students will accept the added work that might follow a change in a committee members. Expect that students will be responsive to the reasonable timelines and expectations of the committee.
Ongoing	Emerge from a doctoral program as "published."	Expect that students will keep the committee chair informed about research or publication opportunities that arise.
Ongoing	Expect frequent access to program committee chairs during the dissertation period.	Be kept abreast of student progress or lack thereof.
Ongoing	Expect a role model for ethical conduct.	Expect that students will act in a manner congruent with the highest ethical standards of research as well as those values enshrined in the NASW Code of Ethics.
After graduation	Expect their program committee chairs to work with them after they complete their dissertations.	Be kept informed about former students' research interests.

Source: Adapted from Schneiderjans, M. (2007). A proposed PhD student bill of rights. *International Journal of Doctoral Studies, 2,* 2–8.

same manner one pursues the dissertation. This is an issue best addressed by research. It is important to consult the literature (e.g., the graduate student handbook), articulate a statement of the problem (e.g., need an effective supervisor), develop or adapt a theory (e.g., there are certain qualities that will make one person more effective than others), frame the question (who will that be?), identify sources of data both formal and informal, collect data, think critically, and consult throughout (e.g., other students, faculty, and colleagues).

EXHIBIT 2.1 STUDENT SELF-INVENTORY

Personal

- Are you fully committed to the dissertation endeavor?
- Do you have the resources that you need?
- Are your personal circumstances congruent with the demands of doctoral studies?

Topic Area

- Do you have a working familiarity with the appropriate background material and seminal pieces in your area?
- Do you have a working familiarity with the important literature in your topic area?
- Do you have a working familiarity with literature/library research technology?
- Have you started to build a personal library of relevant literature?

- Do you have a working familiarity with the works of the major authors in the field?

Methodology

- Do you have a working familiarity with the common research designs used in your topic area?
- Do you have a working familiarity with sampling techniques?
- Do you have a working familiarity with the issues of measurement and instrument development? What other research skills do you need to learn to complete your dissertation research?

If you do not have a working familiarity with any of the above, you may wish to investigate further before preparing a proposal.

Data Analysis

- Do you have a working familiarity with the commonly used data analytic techniques in your area?
- Do you have a working familiarity with the major assumptions underpinning the major data analytic techniques and procedures of interest, and potential analytic procedures to compensate for their violation?
- Are you conversant in the limitations of the statistical analytic procedures you will be using?
- Do you have a working familiarity with appropriate quantitative (e.g., SPSS, SAS) and qualitative data analytic computer programs (e.g., NUDIST)?
- Can you manipulate data appropriately within these programs?
- How much more do you need to learn about these topics to complete your dissertation research?

Writing/Editing

- How good a writer are you?
- What kind of feedback have you had from faculty about your written work?
- Do you have a working familiarity with the writing style required in your school (is it APA, Chicago style, other)?
- Are you comfortable analyzing and synthesizing contradictory findings, both in the literature and your own research?
- As you look at your responses to the questions above, consider whether you need to identify an editor or writing resource to help with revising drafts of the dissertation.

When you have determined exactly what you need from a supervisor you will then go out and pick the perfect match for your needs. Of course, if you believe this to be true, you may need to refine your critical thinking skills. It may be this simple at Ideal U., but at Regular Old U. no matter what your needs are, there may be only one prospective chair available. If so, time spent on your self-inventory is not wasted. You still have to recruit a committee, and the information you have about yourself will be helpful in that task, too. In all likelihood you were going to inherit that supervisor anyway. Now at least you know more about your own strengths and weaknesses and have a platform for discussion about how you get your needs met.

PRELIMINARY MAPPING OF YOUR DISSERTATION TOPIC

Important questions in approaching doctoral studies include where to study, what to study, who to guide you through the process. We assume that you have already decided where to study and are ensconced in a school of social work. The next two questions are closely linked and usually do not proceed in a sequential or linear manner. We suggest having a broad sense of the question that you would like to address, for example, client group (e.g., victims/survivors of domestic violence, HIV-positive youth, Alzheimer's sufferers), level of intervention (e.g., individual, family, group, community), type of study (policy analysis or experimental design), type of intervention (cognitive-behavioral, psychodynamic, task-centered) before you begin to search for a supervisor. Having such a broad sense of your dissertation area can help focus your search for faculty with similar research interests.

As well as these similar interests, there is much other information that you require to make an informed decision. Table 2.3 provides an outline of some suggested sources of information useful in choosing a

Table 2.3 Sources of Information to Support Dissertation Decision Making

	Formal	Informal
People	Faculty advisor, Director of doctoral program	Other students, alumni, staff, faculty
Documents	Graduate student handbook School and university policies and procedures books, journals	Your own notes
Electronic/ Digital	School Web pages, Previous dissertations, Digital library research	Doctoral blogs Other Web resources: Facebook, MySpace, Ratemyprofessors.com
Personal	Grades, Instructor feedback	Self-inventory
Other	Seminars for doctoral students in the school of social work and in other programs	Family and friends (who may know you and your needs very well)

dissertation chairperson. As with all decisions that must be reached throughout the dissertation process, we suggest that you frame the issue, collect evidence, think critically, and consult.

INFORMATION SOURCES

In collecting information about prospective supervisors it is helpful to find out the rules in advance. Who can act as a supervisor in your department? Must they possess a PhD, graduate faculty status (special status at some universities that is required to chair a dissertation), be beyond pretenure review, employed at the school for at least 2 years? What are the procedural criteria to serve in this role? You will also have questions about structure, support, expertise, level of attention available, interpersonal style, teaching style, and so forth. How can you find out? What resources are available to help you decide? Prior consultation and research may help avoid wasting time and energy cultivating a potential supervisor who may not be eligible to act in that capacity.

Consulting the sources in Table 2.3 may reduce, though not eliminate, uncertainty in making many of your dissertation decisions, including the choice of supervisor. When collecting information it is important to utilize both formal and informal sources. Formal sources should always include the PhD handbook, graduate school handbook, university, and school policies and procedures, and associated Web pages. In addition, seminars, presentations, or a course for aspiring doctoral students and candidates may be helpful. Books like this one might be of assistance, too. One useful piece of advice is to make the doctoral student handbook, graduate handbook, or equivalent your friend and make sure that you have the most up-to-date version. It is important to have a version of these items from the time you entered the program as well as current versions. If there is some later dispute or misunderstanding about what is required, it is helpful if you can point to the handbook and say that you followed the relevant written departmental, graduate school, or university procedures. In examining these different sources, be aware that written and electronic sources of information are often out of synch with each other. Some schools focus on updating the Web pages with most recent information, but that may contradict what is in the printed handbook. Others may neglect to keep Web pages up-to-date. It would not be a unique experience to discover that School of Social Work and Graduate School policies are not consistent with each other. If this happens, you should raise it with your supervisor or the director of the doctoral program and ask for clarification.

Informal sources of information include students, faculty, staff, and alumni. In collecting information from informal sources, we recommend that you talk to potential supervisors, other students, and other faculty, and access the institutional memory of many departments vested in the administrative staff. You may also consider consulting your family and friends about what factors they believe you might consider in your decision making; after all, they may know you best.

Some of the questions to which you may need answers include the following. Is there a fit between what you expect from the supervisor and what she expects from you? For example, if she only wants to check drafts of your work at specific points, but you are hoping for more constant feedback, there is a potential mismatch that you need to discuss.

Does she have sufficient expertise in your area of research? Does she have sufficient methodological expertise? What level of skill does she possess in relation to the universal tasks required of a supervisor and those you have identified as specific to you and your circumstances? It is also important to ask her how she sees her role. Having conducted your self-inventory you should now have a better sense of the attributes most important to you in a dissertation supervisor. Ultimately, your dissertation chair may be friendly, but she is not your friend. As the saying goes, if you are looking for a friend, get a dog. If you are looking for a dissertation supervisor, look for someone who can help you through the process.

SUPERVISOR SELECTION

It would be helpful to know at this stage to what extent your prospective chairperson's values mirror your own, especially concerning your education and professional development. For example, we assume you value quality or you would not be subjecting yourself to a doctoral program. Does your value of quality allow for the possibility of hours writing multiple drafts of "straightforward content" because your chair values precision in the use of language? If the search for this level of precision has not been required of you in any previous educational program, will you still value quality so highly? Of course, in making your decision, you also want to know whether your prospective supervisor has the skills to be effective in the role.

According to Schniederjans, "Ph.D. students interact with many educators throughout their educational programs from grade school through the Ph.D. It is with the committee chair that a student will more than likely have the most intense, and therefore, most memorable experiences" (2007, p. 7). An informed choice at this stage may help increase the chances of these being positive as well as "memorable experiences."

In a study that examined supervisor selection, Ray (2007) found the supervisors' perceived "commitment and involvement" in the research work and perceived capacity or willingness to "take a stand" were held highest in importance for both senior and junior postgraduate students. The senior students valued the supervisors' ability to "take a stand" more than "commitment and involvement." Interestingly, the junior students, ranked the items the other way around. Ray suggests that this difference may arise from the increased confidence accruing to senior students who are further along in the research process and thus potentially more confident in their own ability. Ray's research was carried out in a management institute in India and thus the results may not be generalizable to social work doctoral programs in the United States. What this research does suggest, however, is that the value applied to supervisor attributes may change over time. So perhaps what you want to look for is a degree of sensitivity from your supervisor to student maturation and the development of the relationship as well as a degree of flexibility needed to adapt responses to your changing needs.

Selection Criteria

Formal tasks for the committee chair may vary from school to school but there are some universals. Typically, the chairperson will help you select a specific topic, help develop the research problem and methodology, and provide quality assurance before you share the dissertation or chapter drafts with the rest of the committee. This latter implies the requirement that the supervisor actually reads, evaluates, and critiques multiple drafts of each chapter. Besides this, the chair provides all necessary approvals for the dissertation proposal and final dissertation drafts before they are formally submitted to the rest of the committee.

Selection criteria for committee chairs may be broken down into several different areas: academic (educational and subject matter expertise), administrative, personal, and practical. The following discussion highlights some of the issues that we believe are important to consider in your choice of chairperson. In looking at the attributes, it is helpful to examine the role and tasks that fall to the typical dissertation chair.

Supervisor Attributes

Academic: Educational

The characteristics that make somebody a good lecturer may not be the characteristics that make somebody a good supervisor. Teaching is not the same as using the pedagogical principles of adult learning and individual mentorship to facilitate doctoral student learning. This is also true of research skills. It is not enough that your prospective chair be a good researcher; she needs to be willing and able to pass those skills on to you.

Academic: Subject Matter Expert

We believe the advantages of having a supervisor with expertise in your area far outweighs possible disadvantages in other areas but recommend that you factor all areas into your decision making. The advantages include the following. She knows and can direct you to the literature past and present, saving you time and costly mistakes. She will be familiar with common methodological issues and designs for research in your area. She is more likely to be motivated by and interested in your research. You may be able to spin off a dissertation from a larger study of your supervisor's. She may also know other experts in your field and thus be able to help not only your dissertation progress but also your later job search. The disadvantages may include an expectation that you do as you are told because, after all, this is her area of expertise. Such an approach may become an issue if it does not allow you to develop research skills that you will need in your future career. Another possible disadvantage in selecting a content area specialist may be limited opportunity for growing independence that is so necessary in the semiautonomous entrepreneurial world of academia.

If you are planning to seek funding to support your dissertation, you may also wish to factor into consideration the potential chair's overall research experience and her experience specific to your area of interest.

Administrative

In addition to educational skills and content area expertise, the dissertation supervisor's role includes providing administrative oversight of the dissertation and the committee process. For example, your other committee members lead busy professional lives and your research and dissertation may not be their top priority. A good chair will manage the coordination of the other committee members as well as provide reminders to ensure that you are satisfying the bureaucracy's requirements and deadlines. To fulfill these functions your supervisor will need good committee management skills, as she will be responsible for chairing committee meetings and the defense of your proposal and final dissertation. She will need good time management skills to get her comments, edits, suggestions, and recommendations back to you promptly. She will also need to be able to nudge along the glacially paced bureaucracy that characterizes most, if not all, universities. Also remember, just like your responsibilities will change over time, her responsibilities will also change over time as your working relationship matures and develops. Moreover, because social work research typically requires work with vulnerable populations, it is helpful to have a chair with the administrative expertise to help guide you through your university's institutional review board (IRB). Note that though some universities refer to the IRB as a human subjects review board, we prefer the former nomenclature.

Interpersonal

As Ray (2007) pointed out, supervisory assertiveness (ability to take a stand) was highly valued by students in his study. Assertiveness may also be important in your supervisor, particularly if there are disputes between members of your committee or if one of your committee members has unreasonable expectations or makes unreasonable demands. In addition, much of social work research involves cross-disciplinary work, with dissertation committees reflecting the interdisciplinary focus. It is helpful to have an appropriately assertive supervisor who can ensure that you stay on task and move ahead in a timely manner while balancing an interdisciplinary committee.

A chair should also have good communication skills. Clarity is crucial when giving written and oral feedback, whether positive or negative. Although your chair is not responsible for fixing your mistakes, she ought to be able to point them out in a fashion that you can understand.

Practical

You may have identified a faculty member with all the prerequisites but she might still be unsuitable for other reasons. There is no guarantee the person you would like as chair will have the time to spend guiding you through the process. It is not just a search for a supervisor who is an excellent researcher, but it is a search for such a researcher who also has the willingness, time, and ability to impart research skills to you. Stories abound of students having to book appointments with their chair 6 weeks in advance to work on even the smallest of details. At the other end of the continuum from the pathologically busy eminent scholar is the new faculty member. Carlin and Perlmutter (2006) suggest there are some distinct disadvantages to selecting a newly minted faculty member to serve as committee chair. She has her own pressures for publication and tenure. Think of the common trap for new social workers who begin by overcommitting to the clients on their small caseload. As the caseload blooms they are unable to deliver on those early commitments, despite their best intentions, because all the apparent spare capacity has evaporated.

An important consideration then is a practical one. How available is your supervisor going to be during your dissertation process? Is she going on sabbatical, or taking 3 days a week off campus to finish a major piece of work? Is she coming up for tenure and will be very involved/invested in her own work? Is she looking for another position, or near retirement? Does she have an active clinical practice, consulting demands, or research and other academic demands that keep her off campus for long periods of time? Is she tied up on campus with university responsibilities or other faculty governance activities? Is she leaving the country to engage in 6 months of research on itinerant Romany travelers in Eastern Europe? If she has a 9-month faculty appointment, will she be around during the summers, and if so, will she be able to work with you on your dissertation?

Summers are seen as an excellent time for one's own research and scholarship. Even in this age of instant communication, faculty may not maintain connectedness if they are involved elsewhere. Further, how many other students are working with your prospective chair? Is this a person who will have multiple students competing for her time? Will that be okay with you? There is a simple way to find out the answers to these and many other questions: ask; but do so tactfully because some of these issues may be personal or confidential. We are not suggesting that you interview prospective chairs as if they are job applicants, though in some respects they are. We are suggesting that selecting a chairperson is one of the more important aspects of moving from PhD student to PhD holder; and as professional social workers, you are able to ask cogent, salient, sometimes intrusive questions in a professional, respectful manner, without impersonating the Grand Inquisitor.

Other questions to consider include these:

- Will you be available for the duration of my dissertation work?
- How long will you typically have my work before it is returned with comments?
- Will the comments be written or verbal?
- How often would you expect to meet with me?
- What are your expectations of students who work with you?
- How many other students are you supervising?
- How many have you supervised?
- How many of them have graduated?

It is also helpful to know whether your potential supervisor has a track record of getting students through the process successfully or has a cohort of forlorn-looking candidates hanging around for an eternity. How many of her advisees have successfully completed their doctoral careers?

WORKING WITH YOUR CHAIRPERSON

Having agreed with a faculty member that she will act as your supervisor, it is time to move on to developing your research problem more explicitly. Although we said earlier the process is not sequential or even unidirectional, it is important to have a clear idea of what you are going to study and how before you finalize the makeup of your committee. It is also important to communicate as much of the detail of your proposed research as you have available to prospective committee members. They are investing in you, just as much as the other way round.

Developing a timeline for your work is another task that you should refine at this stage. This will also be helpful in your conversations with potential committee members because you will be able to identify the periods when your work will be available to review and when most of their work will occur.

Suggested items for a proposed timeline include these:

- A tentative schedule of meetings
- Date range for your proposal defense
- Dates of data collection and data analysis
- Dates of draft submission
- Date range for completion of final draft
- Date of dissertation submission; deadline for graduation (may be several months before graduation)
- Date range for dissertation defense
- Date of your graduation party!

In the best of circumstances you are in the process of developing a long working relationship with your supervisor, which may go well beyond your time in the doctoral program. You may be wondering what is in it for the supervisor. Why would somebody want to take on such a potentially labor-intensive task? There is a quid pro quo relationship between the supervisor and student in maintaining a relationship even after the student has graduated. Satisfaction with the role of mentor increases as the relationship continues (Erdem & Ozen, 2003), and without this follow-up mentoring, there is evidence that the contribution of younger PhDs is reduced (Walker et al., 2006).

It is helpful to collaborate in a constructive and evolving relationship on work directly connected to your dissertation. It is also important to spend time on work not directly connected to your dissertation but focused on your broader development as a professional. "This degree is more than just taking a series of courses and checking off a list of boxes. Instead, it forms the fundamental grounding for an academic career" (Grover, 2007, p. 12). Consequently, collaboration on presentations, grant proposals, and especially publications, though not directly targeted at your dissertation completion, is very useful in the process of becoming an accomplished academic. On this note, to be competitive in the academic arena, it is increasingly important that you graduate with articles in press if not already published. Of course, if you want to graduate with articles in press, you may want to find a chair with a good track record of publication.

There is an apocryphal story that David Brinkley once said, "A successful person is one who can lay a firm foundation with the bricks that others throw at him or her." In other words, do not take criticism personally; use it wisely to shape, craft, and improve your work. This is useful advice in working with your supervisor, one of whose tasks it is to provide you with sufficiently cogent criticism that you can develop as a researcher. Other considerations in working with your supervisor are these:

- Keep her informed throughout the process.
- Determine when it is appropriate to send drafts.
- Allow enough time for her to read and respond to multiple drafts.
- Determine how polished drafts have to be (e.g., rough or refined) before they are submitted.
- Be realistic about what your responsibilities are and how they differ from hers.
- Set up regular meeting times.
- Come prepared to meetings.
- Do not surprise your supervisor. Not everybody likes surprises.

SELECTING COMMITTEE MEMBERS

Now that you have conducted your self-inventory, selected a chair, refined your proposed study, and developed a tentative timeline, you can identify what skill sets are required of your committee and move to recruit members. Before doing so we suggest that, with your supervisor's input or consent, you develop a clear rationale for asking specific faculty members to join your committee. Base your rationale on their special expertise or experience, not their personal characteristics.

Before asking faculty members to serve on your committee it is vital that you have agreement from your supervisor. It is also worth checking with her whether there is a formal or informal protocol for asking other people to serve. This is also true of ongoing contact with committee members. Ask your chairperson if there is a protocol, or if she has preferences about consultation and contact with other committee members on an ongoing basis outside of formal committee meetings. There are times when protocol and preferences must be considered along with other special circumstances. For example, if a committee member offers specific expertise or skill, then it may be important to consult with that member about specific issues outside of formal committee meetings. There are dangers inherent in too much unfettered access to other committee members; one is the danger of triangulation, in which students are tempted to play off committee members against the chair. Another problem might be termed "multiple accountabilities disorder" (Koppel, 2005) in which you are expected to be accountable to committee members individually and their expectations are not congruent with other members' expectations. Therefore, we suggest that contact with other committee members about the dissertation be only with the involvement or with the consent of your supervisor.

Depending on the model prevalent in your school or the norm created by your committee, you may see a locus of control vested in the committee chair or in the committee itself. In the former, control of the dissertation product and decisions about its release to other committee members are vested in the supervisor. In the latter, there is a more fluid approach to decision making. In the former, it is usual that the proposal and completed dissertation draft are not shared with the committee until the advisor grants approval to do so. This means that methods, hypotheses, research design, measures, and data analytic strategy are developed in consultation with the advisor unless a member or members are invited to share their specific expertise. Where the locus of control is vested more broadly in the committee, there is a less formal control over who reads what when, and again more danger of triangulation and multiple accountabilities. Another consideration may be the level of comfort that prospective committee members have with the chair's locus of control.

WHO CAN SERVE ON A COMMITTEE (OR WHO SHOULD I SELECT TO SERVE ON MY COMMITTEE)?

Just as in selection of your chair, when selecting committee members you are looking for people who can help you maximize opportunities to express your values. To what extent do you see each member contributing to or detracting from these? How congruent are prospective committee members' values with yours in relation to social work, research, and your dissertation? Do you need someone strong in theory, data analysis, methodology, cultural expertise, editing? You can use the Student Self Inventory at the end of this chapter to examine where your greatest needs lie. If you recognize that you are comfortable writing and editing but very inexperienced in data analysis or methodology, then you can factor this into your deliberations about what you need in your committee. Similarly you may wish to consider what you need from a committee that is not available from your supervisor.

As with the selection of your supervisor, it is important to know what the departmental policies are on the selection of committee members. Who is eligible and under what circumstances? Your supervisor should be able to advise you, but you should check in the graduate student handbook or equivalent. You will want to know, for example, if committee members must be graduate faculty, active current researchers, in possession of a Ph.D., tenure track, 2 years post hire. In addition, you should determine program requirements for committee selection (e.g., is graduate school or program director approval of committee members required?).

The exact size, roles, functions, and makeup of committees varies from school to school and every school has its own distinctive culture and policies, but selecting your committee should be based on the skills and needs that you and your advisor bring. In addition you may also wish to consider choosing someone with a reputation for being a good committee member.

Balance and diversity contribute enormously to the quality of the research process but it is not appropriate to ask people to be a member of your committee just because of their race or gender, for example. Social work departments tend to be far more diverse than most academic units and selecting somebody for their expertise, skills, and knowledge can still provide the opportunity for a balanced or diverse committee.

Potential committee members will be interested to hear or read about your proposed topic problem, methodology, and timeline for doing the work as well as why you believe they would make a good addition to your committee. What is it about them and or their expertise that you are interested in and what role do you hope they may play in helping you move through the dissertation process? Under ideal circumstances you want them to bring skills that complement those you already have.

Moreover, there is always the political aspect to consider. For example, suppose you have found a faculty member who shares your interests and meets all of the suggested attributes described above, but this person is untenured and may end up in the unenviable position of having to disagree with a more senior faculty member on the committee. Or perhaps this person is tenured but has academic disagreements with other faculty members who may also be on your committee. Carlin and Perlmutter (2006) suggest that departments set minimum requirements for new faculty before they chair committees as well as limiting the number of committees a new faculty member can sit on because of sheer workload. It is the responsibility of all members in a department to protect untenured colleagues and to ensure that students are not put in potentially compromised positions.

Although we believe it important to have a range of different viewpoints represented on your committee, we also recognize that schools of social work are far from perfect. There may be political reasons for avoiding a specific mix of people in your committee. For example, if your chair and a potential committee member have not spoken for 5 years or if they cannot speak to each other without engaging in a war of words, it is wiser to avoid this mix. In our experience, in many if not most situations, the ability of individuals to work together for the good of the student (even those individuals who may have fundamental disagreements) tends to be much greater than the "grapevine" would suggest. However, the political aspects exist and need to be considered.

Finally, remember that a committee is a small group and as in all small groups, group dynamics are sometimes very unpredictable. As a professional social worker, you no doubt have firsthand experience with small group dynamics. If so, then you know to assess (1) the alignment of prospective members' interests with your own and with one another's, (2) their experience, (3) the soundness, clarity, and quality of their advice, (4) their position, role, and stability within the institution, (5) internal and external recognition, and (6) how well they can work together.

ROLE AND TASKS OF THE COMMITTEE

In most cases it is safe to say that committees function to provide useful feedback and advice throughout the dissertation process. They also serve as a secondary quality control mechanism for the study as well as the final dissertation document, and they conduct the oral defense. They are thus both supporters of your research and inquisitors, though for obvious reasons we prefer to consider them quality assurance people.

You should have a clear understanding about when committee members want to see drafts. It is also important to confirm the details of your proposed chronology with your committee to avoid reaching the defense date and discovering no one is available. You also need to consider the following:

- Is there a formal proposal meeting?
- Is there a proposal defense?
- If so, what are the committee's expectations of you regarding the defense?
- What is the chair's expectation of other committee members?
- Are committee members expecting to read multiple drafts of your chapters or do they want to see a penultimate version of the dissertation?

Many schools of social work require an outside member or outside reader to be included in the committee. The outside reader is generally someone from another department at the university but can also be from another university entirely. Again it is important that you are an informed consumer. Talk to your chair, other faculty, students, staff, and consult the Web pages of the various departments from which you may wish to draw a committee member. Find out what this person's role is on the committee. For example, in one program we are familiar with, students are not allowed to set up a dissertation defense without prior written approval of the dissertation from the outside reader.

COMMON MISTAKES MADE IN MANAGING THE COMMITTEE AND HOW TO AVOID THEM

Grover (2007) identified what he saw as the 10 most common mistakes made by doctoral students. We have taken these and folded them into a list of do's and don'ts. We also added a few of our own (See Table 2.4).

Table 2.4 Do's and Don'ts for Doctoral Students

Do not be too reactive.	Do make appropriate trade-offs.
Do seek help.	Do be prepared for committee meetings.
Do build an asset base.	Do keep your supervisor informed of progress or lack thereof.
Do be politically astute.	Do not leave a program too early.
Do create synergy.	Do not hide from your supervisor.
Do carefully evaluate opportunity costs.	Do not be too ambitious.
Do manage your advisor.	Do not waste committee members' time.
Do carefully select your committee members.	Do not fall into a lull (after comps).

Source: Adapted from Grover, V. (2001). 10 mistakes doctoral students make in managing their program. *Decision Line*, *32*(2), 10–13.

In conclusion, selecting a chair and other committee members should be approached with the same diligence that you will accord your dissertation research. If you use this approach in selecting your committee constellation, will you avoid every potential pitfall? Probably not, but you will be well positioned to manage any pitfall that does occur.

ACTION STEPS CHECKLIST

☐ Develop an inventory of your strengths and needs in relation to the proposed project and the process.

☐ Develop a provisional list of required resources.

☐ Develop a tentative map of your proposed dissertation topic.

☐ Develop a tentative timeline including date ranges for major tasks.

☐ Consult all formal and informal sources of information about potential supervisors and committee members.

☐ Write down the criteria that you will use to inform your decision about selecting and approaching a potential committee chair.

☐ Develop a specific rationale for approaching a prospective chair that is based on her expertise and experience.

☐ Write down the criteria that you will use to inform your decision about selecting and approaching potential committee members.

☐ Develop a specific rationale for approaching prospective committee members that is based on their expertise and experience.

☐ Update proposed project, timeline, and resource list.

3

The Literature Review, Theory, Problem Statement, and Hypotheses

---

Where is the wisdom we have lost in knowledge?
Where is the knowledge we have lost in information?

T. S. Eliot (*The Rock*, 1934)

In 2003, a group of doctoral program directors revised the guidelines for social work doctoral programs. The revisions were ultimately approved by the membership of the Group for the Advancement of Doctoral Education (GADE). The guidelines, you will recall from Chapter 1, described the dissertation as "a student-generated work of independent research and scholarship addressing significant, professionally relevant, theoretically grounded questions or hypotheses" (Anastas et al., 2003, p. 10). To revisit the purpose of doctoral education also presented in Chapter 1, "Doctoral education prepares scholars who both understand what is known and discover what is yet unknown" (Walker et al., 2008, p. ix). The two halves of this statement reflect, on the one hand, the discoveries you will make through your dissertation research, and on the other, your understanding of what is known, revealed in your review of the literature. In other words, the generation of knowledge is a process, not merely a product. This process requires that you know the context of your work in order to understand the nuances and implications of what you are doing. Newton, in a letter to Robert Hooke in 1676, wrote, "If I have seen further it is by standing on the shoulders of giants" (Hawking, 2002, p. 725). If this sounds a trifle hyperbolic, it nonetheless accurately describes the accretion of knowledge that is the basis of scientific advance. We all stand on the shoulders of giants.

In this chapter we discuss the first steps in that independent research and scholarship voyage, the literature review. We address the relevance of theory to social work research and provide strategies and tips for completing a literature search; analyzing, synthesizing, and integrating the literature; developing the statement of the problem; and finally writing the literature review. In addition, we focus on developing hypotheses and defining and operationalizing measurable variables.

OBJECTIVES

By the end of this chapter you will be able to

- Evaluate the role and importance of theory in dissertation research.
- Evaluate quantitative and qualitative research articles.
- Develop a statement of the problem.
- Formulate researchable questions.
- Develop directional/falsifiable hypotheses.
- Define and operationalize variables of interest to your study.

TOPICS

- The literature review
- The role and purpose of theory
- Defining researchable questions
- The statement of the problem
- Hypothesis construction
- Types of variable

THE LITERATURE REVIEW: WHAT IT IS
AND WHAT IT IS NOT

If you are reading this and have already completed your coursework and your competency exams, then you will have more than a passing familiarity with writing high-quality academic research papers. This is an advantage because academic research papers and literature reviews contain similar elements. They both require the ability to locate, integrate, synthesize, and apply a large amount of literature. They both require critical thinking as well as the ability to evaluate the literature and critically examine the ideas advanced by the authors, and they both cover a wide range of sources and content areas. Stated differently, they both require a systematic approach to research and a specific structure for the presentation of your response. There are two major differences, however, between traditional academic research papers and the literature review you will be writing for your dissertation.

First, the main focus of an academic paper is the evaluation of someone else's research, scholarship, and ideas rather than a presentation of, and prelude to, your own research. Second, an academic paper typically focuses on a limited number of sources and usually does not require the same exhaustive review of the previous literature that a dissertation literature review requires. Some students become obsessed in their attempt to ensure that they do not leave out a seminal work or the most recent piece of research in their dissertation literature review. Like many obsessions, this one has potential benefits and unintended consequences; obsessively searching the literature means that a comprehensive review of prior work will be the result; an unintended consequence, because it seems like there is always more research that you can find on any given topic, may be to delay a focus on the important task at hand: completing your dissertation!

Despite its size and scope, your literature review should contain a well-reasoned, clearly articulated case for your research, a structured argument that covers the relevant literature, how various pieces of the literature relate to one another and what these relationships mean for your research specifically and for the advancement of social work knowledge in general. The literature review should also be a critique of the literature that analyzes, synthesizes, and evaluates what has gone before, applying it to the work you are proposing to accomplish. In describing the literature review as a critique, we mean a reasoned analysis of the research in the field that identifies the strengths and limitations of the research and scholarship of others. We suggest that you use the universal intellectual standards: clarity, accuracy, precision, relevance, depth, breadth, and logic (see Paul & Elder, 2006); an evaluative framework; and the principle of fairness to analyze the previous scholarship in your topic area and not simply condemn the work of others. It is worth remembering as you conduct your review that mixed results and inconsistent findings across studies present opportunities for further research.

A common question asked by doctoral students is, "How do I know when my literature review is complete?" The answer is multifaceted. One way to think about this is that your review is complete when you and your chair say so. Another way to think about it is that the review is complete when you have reached saturation. In other words, when you are not finding additional material that either enhances the support of a position or detracts markedly from it. A third criterion you might use to decide when the review is complete is when you feel you have presented a case for your research, based on a structured and integrated argument that covers the literature considered relevant to the field.

Some qualitative researchers suggest that the existing literature should be reviewed only after the research is under way in order to allow understanding from the perspective of the participants (e.g., Crabtree & Miller, 1999). Reviewing the published literature before gaining understanding of the participants' perspective, it is argued, may inhibit the researcher's capacity to listen, observe, and remain open to new concepts and ideas. Moreover, Einstein did not always do a review of the literature when publishing his research (see Einstein, 1905), so why should you? We believe that unless you have specific approval from your chairperson to approach your topic differently, it is wise to review the relevant literature thoroughly before as well as during your dissertation research. The inductive approach to research is not necessarily hypothesis driven but dissertation research should still be grounded in the literature.

Demonstration of your knowledge is not the only reason to conduct a thorough review of the literature. It is also necessary to satisfy your chairperson, committee, and the broader academic community that you are capable of analyzing, synthesizing, and critically evaluating the relevant scholarship in your subject area. Besides displaying your diligence, a good literature review also shows where your work fits in by setting it into a historical, theoretical, and methodological context. It shows that your work is original and that you can handle complex, often opposing ideas. It also provides a rationale and justification for your research, shows why your research question is important, allows you to evaluate sources, and advises the reader on the most pertinent or relevant studies. In short, the literature review should tell a story by making a case for why your research is important, explaining how your study will build on what went before, and hypothesizing how the study will contribute to the field.

Conducting a thorough literature review flows naturally into the process of developing your research question. Getting a sense of your subject area requires having enough familiarity with the literature to make judgments about potential research questions. Of course, you will also generate ideas about potential areas for your research from your experience; coursework; preparation for competency exams; and conversations with your chair, fellow students, and other faculty members. Early in your dissertation work you may not want to be too specific. Specificity comes after the literature review.

Even so, as you mull over possible research topics it might be helpful to consider the following. For each possible research question, ask yourself: Is it interesting? Is it important? Is it an answerable question? Is it social work? Are there resources in the school to support this topic? Is it big enough, broad enough in scope? Is it small enough to be accomplished with the time, resources, and skills available? Is it too large or ambitious? Is it too close to home, tied up with personal issues that may get in the way of your objectivity? Is it too far from home, demanding that you become familiar with a whole new range of material? Is it original, has it been done before? Is it scholarly? Is your question clear? Is dissertation grant funding available to support the project? (See Hasche, Perron, and Proctor, 2009, for a very helpful overview of dissertation funding sources and mechanisms.) As you are tossing these questions over in your mind, remember the adage that the best dissertation is a done dissertation. It might be helpful to think of your dissertation like the driver's exam. Once you have passed it you can go where you please, provided you stay on the road and obey the rules.

STRATEGIES FOR THE LITERATURE REVIEW

To write a cognitively sophisticated literature review, it is important to have an organizing framework that provides structure to the finished product. A structured approach is also crucial when you are assessing the quality of research articles. We believe both the evaluation and the finished product are simplified, facilitated, and improved by adopting a systematic approach.

Systematization is even more pressing with the advent of the World Wide Web, which has made for a wider availability of a larger number of academic resources to anyone with Internet access. The downside of this plethora of information is the increased demand to be critical about the source and the content, to sort and screen it. There are several strategies to help you manage this embarrassment of riches. In other books in this research methods series, you will find some very useful strategies, (e.g., Littell, Corcoran, & Pillai, 2008; Thyer, 2008). Although we will not repeat these strategies here, we will briefly discuss an approach you may wish to consider.

Your first task will be to specify your topic in order to narrow your search. Using your critical thinking skills to define defensible inclusion and exclusion criteria for your search will help make the tasks manageable. Criteria may be expressed in terms of the topic, methodology, theoretical model, source, and problem area as well as the key words that you select for your early library search strategy. Write down your search criteria and use them in your literature review. You may also want to share your search strategy with a reference librarian, one who is familiar with social work and databases from other helping professions. Sources often missed are the databases for the health-related professions. An experienced librarian can help you navigate in these somewhat uncharted waters. Remember the literature review should be comprehensive, but it need not include every article ever published on tangentially related topics.

Another literature search strategy is to look for existing literature reviews, including meta-analyses, in your area and select library search themes from these. This strategy will give you the opportunity to see the organization of a final review as well. Just add the word "review" into the search field with your other key terms. One temptation is to restrict your research to material that is available electronically in full text. We recommend that you avoid this tactic; there are many classic books and articles that have not been digitized. The absence of classic literature from your review would be a glaring omission, especially if what seems like old literature to you seems recent or seminal to your committee members. When conducting your review, although it is important to be as up-to-date as possible, it is also important not to lose sight of the significance of classic and older literature. Indeed, some subject matter lends itself to using older material from classic studies. If no current studies have been conducted, older published studies retain their relevance to a topic. (However, if there are no recent studies in your area of interest, you might want to question whether the topic has been sufficiently explored and what if anything you would bring to it that warrants additional research).

The use of electronic databases and the availability of full text articles for direct download has changed the location in which students spend their time. Previous time devoted to being in the library has been supplanted by time in front of a computer monitor, but this does not mean that aimlessly scrolling through Web pages is research, just as meandering along the library corridors is not research. Most databases offer several access points such as author, title, subject, publisher, key word, and so on. When conducting author, title, or subject searches, the system searches according to your instructions. When you enter terms in specific fields, the computer retrieves information from only those fields identified: The Author Search searches only the author fields and so on. Subject fields typically contain Library of Congress subject headings, descriptors, or combined headings; in other words, a controlled vocabulary.

When starting out you may opt to use a keyword search that allows you to use natural language key terms (i.e., everyday language rather than a controlled vocabulary) and locates these terms in the key fields of a bibliographic record. These key fields vary with each database but usually include author, title, subject, call number, publisher, and note fields such as summary or content notes. Use of a keyword search is helpful when you have natural language terms rather than controlled vocabulary terms, or when you wish to combine concepts. Once you have found a record specific to your research topic, look at the subject headings or descriptor fields. These will help identify the relevant controlled vocabulary terms. Once you have identified them, you may use these headings or descriptors in subsequent searches to add depth to your review while targeting clearly relevant material for your dissertation. Unfortunately, a key term in one database may not be the same term used in another. Moreover, the logic of a search strategy may vary from database to database, and each database is limited by the resources it draws upon. As a result, we suggest that you consider the value added by consulting a qualified academic reference librarian who can often be of help in sorting some of the complexities inherent in doing an electronic literature search, especially when you consider that just as social work is your area of expertise, the academic librarian's is library and information science.

There are added searching techniques available in most systems that allow limiting the search parameters by language, media, and date range of publication. Truncation allows you to retrieve records of all variations of a word. Most modern databases will let you use a symbol, which can vary between databases ($, ?, +, #, * are the most common). Thus a search for "psycholog*" will also search for psychology, psychological, psychologist. You can also search for variations within a word. Wom*n for example will acquire women and woman. Boolean operators (AND, OR, NOT) help the computer understand the relationships between terms and will thus allow you to combine, include, or exclude search terms. Databases usually have reference material to help you determine what literature is included and how to structure the language in your search. It is a good idea, if you have not already done so, to become familiar with the key words used by the different professions, databases, and journals to sort scholarly information. Once again, your reference librarian can be very helpful in this regard.

When writing journal articles, authors are invited to submit a short string of key words for use in indexing and searching. These words, typically drawn from a preexisting list, can be found when searching electronically as hypertext links in the retrieved records. Authors' names are also searchable in this way so you can trace the works of authors writing in your area of interest.

Trawling through the references section of articles you have found helpful is another way to uncover useful literature that may have escaped your other search strategies. This strategy also gives the option for both forward and backward searches. A backward search means that you can comb for important literature that predates your current source (otherwise it could not be cited). A forward search arises when you discover authors who are conducting research in your area and you subsequently use their names in a search to find their most recent literature. It is now possible to enter the name of any author into a search engine such as PsycInfo, ERIC, or Web of Science, and a list of published articles by that author will be available.

Social Work Abstracts is a useful resource, particularly for adoption, foster care, and child welfare issues, but it is not as broad as others beyond the profession. Social work research is interdisciplinary and some of the most commonly used databases for social work literature are PsycINFO, Social Services Abstracts, and Sociological Abstracts. In the health fields, Medline and CINAHL are commonly used. In education, ERIC is one of the mainstays; Science Citation Index (SCI), Social Sciences Citations Index (SSCI), and Google Scholar are also useful resources. Do not underestimate your university's library home page as a resource in identifying relevant databases. The trend in recent years has been toward aggregation into commercially available databases accessed through university libraries or other major systems. However, no database should be considered complete or totally comprehensive. The speed with which information technology advances in all fields including information retrieval means that it is unwise to be too specific here, given that such information will be obsolete by the time you read this book.

HOW TO EVALUATE THE LITERATURE

Although the peer review process is not perfect (Dalton, 2001), peer reviewers who evaluate potential publications bring a wealth of individual knowledge and usually make every attempt to ensure that what is published is accurate. Therefore, when reading research, make certain the references are from scientific, peer-reviewed journals and not from general interest magazines or other printed matter that has not been subject to the peer-review process. Some online journals also have peer-review processes. However, despite what some people believe, Wikipedia is not a peer-reviewed publication and should not be used in your literature review. Because peer review is not a perfect process, however, it is incumbent on you to judge the quality and validity of articles. The questions in Checklist 3.1 address the relevance, source,

...ɔrship, ethics, conflicts, article content and structure and are intended to direct your attention to issues that are of importance, whether the article under consideration is based on inductive or deductive research.

CHECKLIST 3.1: QUESTIONS RELEVANT TO BOTH QUANTITATIVE AND QUALITATIVE RESEARCH

- ☐ Did this article relate to my dissertation topic? (If not, put it down). If so, how and where can I use it? (e.g., defining the extent of the problem, applicable theory, useful instruments, etc.).
- ☐ Were there any biases or potential conflicts in the author's background?
- ☐ What were the author's credentials, degrees, professional position, and experience?
- ☐ Did the article match the author's expertise?
- ☐ Was there a clearly defined issue or problem?
- ☐ Was the significance (scope, severity, prevalence, consequences) clearly established?
- ☐ Was there a relevant and comprehensive literature review?
- ☐ Were there counter positions in the literature review?
- ☐ If so, how were they handled?
- ☐ Was there a statement about potential conflict?
- ☐ Was IRB or human subjects approval mentioned?
- ☐ Who was in the sample?
- ☐ How was the sample selected?
- ☐ Was the sample appropriate to answer the research question?
- ☐ Were the methods used for recruitment described in enough detail?
- ☐ What was found?
- ☐ Were the results meaningful?
- ☐ Did the reported results flow from the hypotheses or problem statement?
- ☐ Were the reported results consistent with the data analysis?
- ☐ Did the conclusions flow from the results?
- ☐ Did you see other conclusions that should be drawn?
- ☐ Did the conclusions flow from the research question?
- ☐ Were there conflicts in or between sections?

☐ Were there inconsistencies?

☐ When you deconstruct the author's argument is it coherent and logical?

A negative answer to any of these questions or a series of questions does not necessarily mean the article should be excluded from your review. It does, however, suggest that you might want to proceed cautiously if you do include it, and be especially tentative about any conclusions you draw from the research.

ANALYZING QUANTITATIVE ARTICLES.

A good deductive scientific research paper addresses a novel and scientifically important subject and has clearly stated hypotheses grounded in the results of previous investigation. Another feature of rigorous research is a study design that includes prior determination of the statistical tests that will be used to analyze the data. Another is to ensure the sample size is large enough to provide enough statistical power to detect results. These are only some of the elements that you should be looking for. We have included below a list of questions to use when analyzing quantitative articles that will help point you to some of the others.

CHECKLIST 3.2: QUESTIONS RELEVANT TO QUANTITATIVE RESEARCH

☐ Was this article published in a research journal publishing the results of original investigations derived empirically using the scientific method?

☐ Was there a theoretical framework, or was the research based on a client or societal problem?

☐ If so, what was it?

☐ Was there an explicit research question?

☐ Did the research question flow from the literature review?

☐ Were there explicit directional hypotheses?

☐ Was there a discussion of statistical power?

☐ Given the information provided could you duplicate this study?

☐ Was the evaluation method planned in advance and linked to the aims of the study?

☐ Were any measures used? If so, were they described in enough detail?

☐ What is your assessment of the study design?

☐ How accurate and valid were the measurements?

☐ Did the research design allow for control of threats to internal, external, and statistical conclusion validity?

☐ If so, what method of control was adopted (e.g., control group, quasi-experiment)?

☐ Were the data analytic techniques appropriate?

☐ Were steps taken to compensate for multiple comparisons?

ANALYZING QUALITATIVE ARTICLES

Most deductive research tends to be quantitative and answers questions that begin, "How many?" or "How much?" Inductive research is usually qualitative and answers questions that begin, "What is?" or "Why?" Sherman and Reid (1994) point to a long tradition of qualitative research in social work (e.g., Hollis, 1949; Richmond, 1917), emphasizing that the early case study method used by Hollis was "a systematic content analysis of the case records" (Sherman & Reid, 1994, p. 2). From these beginnings, the social work literature now contains more and more research based on qualitative models to which many of the criteria used for evaluating quantitative studies do not apply (Shek, Lee, & Tan, 2007; Shek, Tang, & Han, 2005). Though this may vary depending on the inductive approach used, qualitative research typically requires a large degree of interpretation by the researcher. Multiple passes by multiple people through the data are both possible and desirable and typically this leads to multiple interpretations. Thus, reliability and validity do not translate to qualitative research in the same way they are understood in quantitative studies. Some authors refer to credibility and trustworthiness of the data in qualitative research rather than reliability and validity (see, e.g., Shek et al., 2005).

The evaluation of qualitative research requires consideration of the epistemological assumptions underlying the study. Thus, it is important to evaluate the appropriateness of the experimental design to the research being undertaken. In other words, we should evaluate the merits of data collection and analysis within the parameters of the research paradigm chosen by the authors of the study being evaluated.

Building on the work of Mary Richmond (1917), who discussed issues of truth and bias, and despite some opposition to "criteriology" (Padgett, 1998; Reicher, 2000), a number of guidelines for ensuring the rigor and credibility of qualitative research have been identified (Creswell, 1998; Drisko, 1997; Elliott, Fischer, & Rennie 1999; Lincoln & Guba, 1985; Miles & Huberman, 1994; Padgett, 1998; Stiles, 1993; Whittemore, Case, & Mandle, 2001; Willig, 2001; Yardley, 2000). The questions below are adapted from, and to an extent overlap with, those identified by the above authors. The fundamental principle underlying these criteria is that qualitative research should be carried out in a way that is systematic and rigorous.

CHECKLIST 3.3: QUESTIONS RELEVANT TO QUALITATIVE RESEARCH

- ☐ Was there a clearly specified research objective?
- ☐ Was a clear methodology identified?
- ☐ If so, did it flow from the research objectives?
- ☐ Did sample selection flow from the study objectives?
- ☐ Did claims to generalizability flow from the study philosophy, objectives, and sample?
- ☐ Were biases identified and addressed in a manner consistent with the study philosophy and objectives?
- ☐ Did the study analysis, conclusions, and recommendations flow from the study philosophy, objectives, and findings?
- ☐ Were any credibility checks used? If so, what were they?

Barker and Pistrang (2005) also recommend several criteria and credibility checks for evaluating qualitative research. First, they suggest that since the role of the researcher in qualitative research is central, the researcher should disclose personal background information that may have a bearing on the conduct of the inquiry and subsequent interpretation of the data. Second, they suggest that it is important to provide enough examples of observations to give the reader a clear sense of the researcher's understanding of the data. Third, they suggest it is crucial for the researcher to provide a consistent, systematic, and logically coherent structure in which to present the ideas induced from the data. Shek, Tang, and Han (2005) recommend their own set of guidelines to enhance qualitative research. First, the philosophical base for the study needs to be clearly described. Second, the researcher should provide a clear description of sample recruitment and data analysis. Third, special attention needs to be paid to the possibility for bias. Fourth, the researcher should pay special attention to "truth value (e.g., triangulation, peer checking, and member checking) and consistency, such as reliability and audit trails" (p. 192). Finally, researchers should properly consider alternative explanations and negative cases.

Several credibility checks have also been proposed (Elliott et al., 1999; Miles & Huberman, 1994; Padgett, 1998; Stiles, 1993), and though one might not expect all of these to be present in every qualitative study, there should be at least some evidence of attempts to ensure trustworthiness. The first credibility check for our purposes is centered on consensus, achieved by using a team of researchers to analyze the data jointly rather than relying on a single analyst. The second check is auditing, carried out by having another researcher (not directly involved in conducting the study) examine an "audit trail" provided by the investigator. Third, respondent validation can be carried out by asking the research participants themselves to comment on the researcher's interpretations. Fourth is triangulation, performed by establishing whether the findings are consistent with those derived from other methods or sources. There are obvious commonalities across each set of credibility recommendations. What is essential, however, is that the quality of qualitative research, just like quantitative research, deserves rigorous scrutiny.

HOW TO WRITE A LITERATURE REVIEW

Chapter 7 of this book provides some guidance about writing your dissertation. It is important at this stage, however, to touch on the cognitive complexity that you should aim for in all of your writing, including the literature review. Granello (2001) described the use of the 1956 version of Bloom's Taxonomy (Bloom, 1956) to improve the quality of literature reviews. Although there are critics of the hierarchical nature of the taxonomy (Paul, 1993), and the order has been rearranged recently (Anderson & Krathwohl, 2001), we believe the principles outlined by Granello provide useful guidance. The taxonomy describes increasing levels of cognitive complexity including at the lower level knowledge, ranging through comprehension, application, to analysis, synthesis, and evaluation.

Writing at the level of evaluation contains elements from all the other levels but would also reflect the ability to determine the quality of source material in the context of the material's original purpose. At the evaluation level your writing should reflect the use of defined criteria in making judgments. Where those criteria exist you should adopt them, but in their absence you should develop your own. Writing at this level also reflects distinctions between empirically derived research and conceptual material, anecdote, opinion, or experience. Using skills acquired from your research courses you will make evaluative comparisons between research articles and be able to accommodate contradictory research results.

By now you will have a clear sense that an annotated bibliography is not a literature review, so you will know that simply listing your sources and describing them one at a time is not appropriate for dissertation-level work. You have to bring critical thinking and structure to your reading in order to decide which are the most important topics and how they break down into subtopics. You also have to decide in what order you wish to present the material.

There are many different ways to order your literature review. You could adopt a chronological approach based on the time period the material was published. We recommend that if you adopt this approach you group by specific time periods—from the 1940s to the early 1950s, for example, or by decade or some other meaningful breakdown of time. This approach is appropriate as long as it allows for continuity among subjects. Ordering your review by specific publication may also be appropriate but only if the order demonstrates an important trend.

Another way to organize your sources chronologically is to examine the sources under themes. Psychodynamic, behavioral, humanistic, or cognitive-behavioral approaches to understanding human motivation and change, for example, can all be located in specific, though overlapping, time periods. It is often possible, given their theoretical orientation, to tell not just where somebody went to school but also when.

Moving away from chronology altogether, you could adopt a more broadly thematic organizing structure around a topic or issue. This type of review may shift between time periods within each section according to the material presented. Methodology is one of the potential themes in which the focusing factor is not the content of the material but rather the methods of the researcher. This type of organizing structure has an impact on both the way material is discussed and on the material selected for review.

Once you have opted for an organizing framework, the outline for your review will become clear. The headings will arise out of your organizational strategy. Even so, you may choose additional headings or subheadings that do not fit into the organizational strategy. These may include the current situation, recent developments, or the history of the topic, which in a thematic review are often helpful to provide context. You may also opt to use particular standards; for instance, you might explain that your review includes only peer-reviewed articles and journals, and then divide these by level of methodological rigor, from the strongest to the weakest.

THE ROLE AND PURPOSE OF THEORY

Social work is at the intersection of many disparate fields: psychology, sociology, medicine, law, politics, social policy, to name a few; thus, you may draw on appropriate theoretical models from many disciplines. There are many social work theories that have either been adapted for social work from these other disciplines or have grown up within social work itself. An excellent book on theory in social work is Malcolm Payne's *Modern Social Work Theory* (2005). Some of the topics covered in this book are the psychodynamic perspective, crisis intervention, task-centered casework, cognitive-behavioral, systems, ecological perspectives, humanism, existentialism, social and community development, and radical and critical perspectives. All of these provide theoretical frameworks that are the basis for our understanding of how social work actually works.

As is the case in many other disciplines, however, the role of theory in social work research has been the subject of debate. On the one hand, there are those who view the emphasis on theory as problematic (e.g., Thyer, 2001); on the other are those who see theory as essential (Gomory, 2001a, 2001b). These contrasting views are reflective of an early distinction made by Mary Richmond: "in social study, you open your eyes and look, in diagnosis, you close them and think" (1917, p. 347). The extent to which you open your eyes and look or close them and think is a matter for discussion with your chair, but it is a matter that should be discussed early in your dissertation process.

Theories have several basic functions; they are used to describe, to explain, and to predict. The role of theory in your dissertation is to provide an organizing framework through which you conduct your study. In addition, your dissertation research can make a contribution to the confidence we have in a particular theory or to our understanding of the conditions under which the theory coheres.

Given its mandate to improve the living conditions of vulnerable people, social work may be viewed as an applied social science. As a result, social work research at the dissertation level and beyond is often concerned with solving practical social problems. Without a theoretical or systematic framework to guide research, however, there is a danger of a slide into "mindless empiricism." Dissertation research should be concerned with more than problem resolution; as Kerlinger and Lee (1999) suggest, "the basic purpose of scientific research is theory" (p. 5). This can be a difficult stance for social workers to adopt, even those pursuing doctoral level research.

As a research question, asking "Are more male or female children physically neglected?" is of little consequence without a theoretical framework to help conceptualize why this should be so. One of the contexts that your review of the literature provides for your research is the theoretical connection between variables of interest. This connection allows you to make tentative predictions and test how robust the theory may be.

Although using a theoretical framework is fundamental to making connections between variables, the use of explanatory theories is often a stumbling block for experienced social workers who are novice social work researchers. The former have been socialized to solve practical social problems, to fix things. A research dissertation should contribute to scholarship, however, not simply fix something. Fixing is important but it is not enough on its own to merit a dissertation. Here is a practical reason for encompassing theory that may satisfy the social work need to fix problems. If your dissertation research solves a practical social problem, absent a theory to explain why your approach worked, you cannot know if it was your intervention that made the difference (Monroe, 2002). In describing how one might go about evaluating intervention outcomes, Bloom, Fischer, and Orme (2006) suggest that the social worker look at practical/clinical, statistical, and/or theoretical significance. Their suggestion helps to bridge the gap between rigor and relevance.

Balancing rigor and relevance is one of the tensions inherent in social work research as in many other fields. Often this is a false dichotomy, however, and the two are not mutually exclusive. It is important in a dissertation to carry out rigorous systematic research underpinned by an appropriate epistemology or theory. This does not mean that your dissertation cannot address a practical problem. It does mean that you have to have a theoretical framework to explain your theory of change.

Educational researcher Frederick Kerlinger (1957) fought against practicality in research. From his perspective, there simply was no such thing as a practical answer to a practical question. He believed that "all questions have behind them theoretical foundations without the exploration of which the questions are impossible to answer" (p. 36). He warned against proclaiming the position that the purpose of research was collecting data. He saw the purpose of research as theory building and testing.

In a professional field such as social work, this position may seem both privileged and difficult to defend; even so, it should not be dismissed. In their study of dissertation research in public administration, management, planning, criminology, women's studies, and social work, Adams and White (1994) proposed six indicators of dissertation quality—two of which were concerned with theory.

- Research was on a researchable topic of some potential value to the field.
- Research was guided by some explicit theoretical or conceptual framework.
- Research was relevant to theory and could contribute to theory development.
- Research has practical relevance within the research setting. It could have helped change or improve something in that setting.

- Research has practical relevance beyond the research setting. Something could have been learned that might inform practice in another setting.
- There are no serious flaws in the research (e.g., sample too small to draw reasonable conclusions, generalization of findings from a single case study, use of an inappropriate statistic, blatant errors in logic, inappropriate research design given the research problem, serious misapplication of some theory to the research problem).

HOW TO RECOGNIZE AND DEFINE RESEARCHABLE QUESTIONS

A straightforward way to begin thinking about researchable questions is to address the who, when, where, what, how, and why of issues important to social work. You may use various permutations of these questions to define the context of your research. Do seniors (who) live in supported accommodations (where) have less contact (what) with their external support network? Do child witnesses (who) of domestic violence (what) display different affective and behavioral outcomes (what) than child (when, how old) victims of physical abuse (what)? Asking these questions can then lead to others. Your literature review may reveal the answers to the questions raised above, and you may then add another level of complexity by asking under what circumstances (how) and by what mechanism (when, why, and how) this difference occurs.

Essentially you are engaged in the search for variability and the conditions under which variability occurs. Looking at the next level of questions adds a layer of complexity often by adding a third variable. For example, in the senior question raised above you may want to introduce proximity as a third variable. Does the distance between the senior complex and the support network contribute to some variability? In the child maltreatment example you may wish to include maternal support as a third variable. Does the response of the child's mother to domestic violence or child maltreatment contribute to variability in outcomes for the child? Each of these new questions has the potential to add new variables to the mix.

Another productive way to identify research questions is to ask experts in the field. Whether you ask them in person or interrogate their writings is a matter of opportunity. Published research agendas are another possible source for research question generation that taps into expertise. Many of these are available, for example, in gerontology (Morrow-Howell & Burnette, 2001), palliative and end of life care (Kramer, Christ, Bern-Klug, & Francoeur, 2005), suicide prevention (Joe & Niedermeier, 2006), child sexual abuse (Kerns, 1998), quality of care (McMillen et al., 2005), health care ethics (Jansson & Dodd, 1998), and violence against women (Bell, 2004). Agency funding priorities are also fertile ground for ideas.

Developing Qualitative Questions

Depending on the orientation of your school and chair, there may be a greater or lesser willingness to entertain qualitative dissertations. Writing a brief concept paper that presents your proposed research as well as your proposed methodological approach can not only be helpful in focusing your thinking but can also help in determining your committee's willingness to entertain a particular methodological approach.

Typically, qualitative research seeks to answer questions about why people behave the way they do, how opinions and attitudes are formed, how personal understanding of events are shaped. It is concerned with finding the answers to questions that begin with "Why?" "How?" and "In what way?" The differences between quantitative and qualitative research are not just in the first interrogatory, however; qualitative research seeks a depth of personal understanding beyond that sought in quantitative research. Qualitative researchers might ask, for example, How, or in what ways do women's approaches to community building differ from men's? Why do they differ? How do refugees and displaced persons make sense of their experiences? What does it feel like to suffer from obsessive-compulsive disorder?

Qualitative research is often undertaken to describe or understand particular situations, answering questions about experiences and meanings before developing and testing more general theories and explanations. In circumstances where "linear causality does not apply," qualitative methods allow "transactional explanations of causality" (Sherman, 1994, p. 159); thus, qualitative research designs are often emergent and need to be flexible. The use of inductive reasoning suggests that what is learned in the early stages of research has consequences for what comes later. Qualitative studies should answer clearly stated, important research questions (Frankel & Devers, 2000), and when there are well-developed theoretical and conceptual frameworks and much is already known about the topic, defining the specific question is not a major problem. Your literature review may have helped you identify your primary research question. However, a clearly specified problem is not always easily identified, and in some areas qualitative research may be conducted just to find out what the right questions might be. In addition, qualitative research is often nonlinear and non-sequential, but this does not mean that you should launch into a qualitative research project without having a clear idea of what your initial research question is.

In defining your research question, whether qualitative or quantitative, you can test it against several criteria.

- Interest: Are you sufficiently interested in finding the answer to the question to complete the research? Will it hold your interest during your dissertation and beyond? (If not, we recommend finding another topic. Dissertations can be arduous and should not be approached lightly if you are one day to be called "Doctor.") Does the topic offer you a research trajectory? Can you mine the topic for years to come?
- Importance: Will the answer to the question make a difference?
- Generalizability: Will the answer to the question make a difference to social workers, social work researchers, and clients beyond your sample?
- Feasibility: Can the question be answered by your research project, or indeed by any research project? (Morrison, 2002)

Developing Quantitative Questions

Once you have defined your research question and decided that it meets the above criteria and you know from your literature review that it has not been answered by somebody else, the next steps are to formalize your statement of the problem, develop your hypotheses, identify and operationalize the variables of interest, and then decide on the methods you wish to employ to address the question. If the question is precisely focused, determining the best method of inquiry becomes much easier.

The Statement of the Problem

Your dissertation should be a penetrating analysis of a limited problem rather than a superficial examination of a broad area. The steps in defining your problem statement thus become more and more precise. You probably started out with a broad idea of the topic area in which you would like to conduct your research. This broad idea will have become more focused as you progressed through the coursework in the first stage of your doctoral program, becoming even more refined as you selected your dissertation chair. Then, working with the chair you may have developed a precise topic area culminating in a specific statement of the problem. Questions to consider are these:

- Does this statement of the problem lead to a researchable question?
- Is there a relationship to be examined?
- Is the relationship testable?
- Can the variables be defined operationally?
- Is the research feasible given the resources you have (e.g., Access to subjects, data, agencies)?

Hypothesis Construction

Hypotheses should be clear, unambiguous, concise, and meaningful. They should also describe testable relationships between two or more variables. Here is a place to remember some of the material that you learned in your first practice class.

- Do not ask ambiguous questions.
- Do not ask double-barreled questions.
- Do not ask leading questions.

All of these admonitions apply to hypothesis construction. Do not develop ambiguous hypotheses—for example, Communities with greater social cohesion show different resident satisfaction with social work services. Do not develop double-barreled hypotheses—men who engage in violence toward their partners have poor impulse control and are more likely (than whom?) to have a history of being maltreated as a child. Do not pose biased hypotheses—obviously male recipients of intervention X will achieve better outcomes than female recipients. To adopt guidelines from the universal intellectual standards, your hypotheses should be clear, accurate, precise, relevant, and logical.

To convert your research question into hypotheses, start out with your question and then develop a clear, precise, specific prediction about the relationship (or lack thereof) between the variables of interest. For example, a research question might ask, How do disaster survivors cope with the aftermath of their experiences? Hypotheses that derive from this broad question might include the following:

- H1: Disaster survivors make increased use of formal support systems compared with their presurvivor status.
- H2: Disaster survivors make increased use of informal support systems compared with their presurvivor status.

Converting research questions into hypotheses need not be a daunting task. Take your research questions and turn them into positive statements that say either a relationship exists, which would lead to a correlational study, or a difference exists, which would lead to an experimental study. To create a null hypothesis, simply change your statement to read that a relationship does not exist or a difference does not exist.

- Research Question for Relationships: Is there a relationship between sexual orientation and level of self-esteem?
- Null Hypothesis: There is no relationship between sexual orientation and level of self-esteem.
- Alternate hypothesis: There is a positive [negative] relationship between sexual orientation and level of self-esteem. The alternate hypothesis is typically also your research hypothesis.

Remember, the null hypothesis is assumed to be true at the beginning of your research. This assumption means that your project is designed on the basis that there is no relationship between variables, or that the differences or associations observed between variables are the consequence of chance alone.

Your review of the literature and your adoption of a theoretical underpinning for your research are useful here. They provide the rationale for making the prediction that you need for your hypotheses. In summary, there are several steps that you take before finalizing your hypotheses. Consult the literature, evaluate the theory, consult your chairperson, and then make your predictions. When you do, you will be making what has been described as a conditional scientific prediction (If X happens, then Y will happen) rather than an unconditional scientific prophecy (Y will happen) (Popper, 2002). For the philosopher of science Karl Popper, a theory is scientific only if it is refutable by a conceivable event. In other words, your hypotheses are falsifiable. A genuine test of your theory is an attempt to refute or to falsify it. One genuine counter instance falsifies the whole theory. Attempted refutation may sound like a tall order, but the corollary is to engage in the logically flawed process of justificationist research—that is, the search for evidence that supports your hypothesis.

It is important that in your prediction there is an indication of the direction of variability you expect or for which you are testing. It is imprecise to devise a hypothesis postulating "a difference." You must ask how it will be different, increased, decreased, larger, smaller, higher, lower, more of, less of, greater frequency, less often.

Hence, if you are looking for change or variability (that's why they are called variables) you should ask yourself what causes the variability. What might explain it? What other potential third variable is lurking here? What theoretical framework might explain the role of this third variable? You may want to draw a picture of your variables and how you see them connected to get a graphic sense of their relationship.

Independent variable: An independent variable, which you will see variously described as the experimental, manipulated, treatment, or grouping variable, is the factor that is measured, manipulated, or selected to determine if and how it is related to an observed phenomenon. Independent variables are antecedent; they come first and are presumed to affect a dependent variable. You manipulate or observe them so their values can be related to the values of the dependent variable (Preacher, Rucker, & Hayes, 2007; Rubin & Babbie, 2007). Although the independent variable may be manipulated—change in dosage or frequency, for example—this is not always the case. It can also be a classification where subjects are assigned to groups. In a study where one variable causes the other to change, the independent variable is the cause.

In a study where groups are being compared, the independent variable is the group.

Moderator variable: A moderator variable is a special type of independent variable, one that influences the strength of a relationship between two other variables. The independent variable's relationship to the dependent variable may change under different conditions. These conditions are the moderator variables. In a study of two interventions for obsessive-compulsive disorder (OCD), one of the interventions may have greater efficacy with males than females. The intervention is the independent variable and OCD symptoms are the dependent variable. Gender is the moderator variable because it moderates or changes the relationship between the independent variable (intervention) and the dependent variable (symptoms) (Baron & Kenny, 1986; Preacher & Hayes, 2008; Preacher et al., 2007).

Mediator variable: Just to add to the confusion, a mediator variable is one that explains the relationship between the two other variables. Take the example of the relationship between social class and risk of HIV seropositivity. Race might be a moderator variable, in that the relation between social class and HIV status may be stronger for minorities. Education might be a mediator variable, in that it explains why there is a relationship between social class and HIV status. When you remove the effect of education, the relationship between social class and HIV status may disappear (Baron & Kenny, 1986; Preacher & Hayes, 2008; Preacher et al., 2007).

Dependent variable: the dependent variable represents the principal focus of your research interest. It is the consequent variable that is or is not affected by one or more independent variables, which are either manipulated or observed by you. The dependent variable is the outcome. In an experiment, it may be what was caused or what changed as a result. In a comparison of groups, it is what they differ on. In other words, it is the factor that appears, disappears, or varies as you introduce, remove, or vary the independent variable.

To measure your variables you must find a way to operationalize them. Operationalization is the process of taking specific concepts and devising empirical measures for those concepts to use as part of your hypothesis testing. The process is iterative and results in developing specific research procedures and measures such as survey questions, experimental protocols, interview schedules, observation protocols, and so on. These in turn result in empirical observations representing your variables in the real world. There are typically three steps in operationalization:

- Formulate your concepts into variables.
- Formulate variables into measures,
- Find or formulate instruments for the measures.

Other issues to consider in respect of the variables in your study are the levels of variable measurement. Typically, four levels of measurement are defined:

- Nominal
- Ordinal
- Interval
- Ratio

In nominal measurement, no ordering of the cases is implied. For example, jersey numbers in sports teams are measures at the nominal level. Number 10 is not more of anything than number 5; neither is it two times the value.

In ordinal measurement, the attributes can be ranked, but distances between attributes do not mean anything. For example, on a risk-assessment instrument you might code risk of maltreatment as 1 = low; 2 = moderate; 3 = high. In this measure, higher numbers mean greater risk, but we cannot know if the distance between 1 and 2 is the same as the distance between 2 and 3.

In contrast, the distance between attributes does have meaning in interval measurement. For example, when we measure temperature, the increase from 20 degrees to 30 degrees is the same amount of increase as from 50 degrees to 60 degrees. The interval between values is interpretable. Thus, it makes sense to compute an average of an interval variable, but not for ordinal scales. In interval measurement, however, ratios do not make any sense; 20 degrees is not twice as hot as 10 degrees even though the value is twice as big.

Ratio measurement always has an absolute zero that is meaningful. Zero degrees Fahrenheit does not mean a complete absence of heat, but 0 inches does mean a complete absence of distance. You can therefore construct a meaningful fraction (or ratio) with a ratio variable. In social work research, most "count" variables are ratio variables (the number of clients). It is important to remember that there is a hierarchy implied in levels of measurement. At the lower levels, assumptions tend to be less restrictive and data analyses tend to be less sensitive. As you move up the hierarchy, the level includes all of the qualities of the one below it and adds something new. Usually it is preferable to have a higher level of measurement (interval or ratio) rather than a lower one (nominal or ordinal).

In summary, the review of the literature is your guide to what has gone before and to what your dissertation may contribute. A systematic and comprehensive literature review will provide the basis for decisions about the role of theory in your research as well as helping you to define your statement of the problem, research questions, and variables of interest.

ACTION STEPS CHECKLIST

☐ Develop a systematic strategy for your literature review.
☐ Define inclusion and exclusion criteria for your search.
☐ Contact a reference librarian for advice.
☐ Search within social work and other related fields.
☐ Identify and clarify the role of theory in your research.
☐ Define and refine your research problems and questions.
☐ Develop a precise statement of the problem.
☐ If appropriate, develop clear, specific, testable, hypotheses.
☐ Identify all variables and classes of variables.

4

Ethics and Research Methodology

A magician pulls rabbits out of hats.
A social scientist pulls habits out of rats.

Anonymous

Some of the most important decisions you will make about your dissertation are concerned with your choice of methodology and research design. In this chapter we will describe quantitative, qualitative, and mixed-methods designs; discuss experimental, explanatory, exploratory, and descriptive research; program evaluation; and the relative merits of disparate models of research, including the requirements of rigor in both quantitative and qualitative studies.

OBJECTIVES

By the end of the chapter you will be able to

- Evaluate the fit between research strategies and problems under investigation.
- Recognize when to use quantitative, qualitative, or mixed methods strategies.

TOPICS

- Ethics in research
- Types of study
- Methods of study: Quantitative research methods
- Methods of control
- Research design
- Threats to validity
- Methods of study: Qualitative research methods
- Methods of investigation
- Grounded theory
- Hermeneutics
- Ethnography
- Participant observation
- Program evaluation

"Investigators must balance their interest in gathering data and answering research questions with society's mandate to protect the rights and safeguard the welfare of research subjects" (NIH, 2004, p. 1). As a dissertation researcher, you are required to balance your research requirements with the well-being and rights of your study participants; however, this level of human subject protection has not always been present. The current system was the result of historical concern about the unethical, inhumane, and overtly cruel treatment of participants in numerous, notorious research projects.

In Nuremberg in 1946, for example, 23 Nazi medical practitioners were tried for crimes committed against prisoners of war. The crimes included mutilating surgery, exposure to extremes of temperature resulting in death, and deliberate infection with deadly organisms. Media attention to the war crimes trials led to widespread public outcry and ultimately to the development of the Nuremberg Code (1949), which was in turn reflected in the United Nations Declaration of Human Rights, and the UN Charter itself. The code spelled out ethical principles for research intended to safeguard the autonomy and well-being of research participants. The World Health Organization (WHO) also later adopted broad guidelines to limit harm to study participants (Weindling, 2004).

Another disturbing example of the unethical treatment of study participants involved the Tuskegee Syphilis Study (1932–1972) in which some 400 African American men had been told that they would be treated for the disease. For four decades, however, the men were unwitting participants in a study of the disease's progress. The men were routinely and systematically refused penicillin treatment, even after the drug became the standard treatment for the disease (Jones, 1981). Revelations about the Tuskegee Study in the 1970s led to passage of the National Research Act of 1974 and to the formation of the National Commission for the Protection of Human Subjects of Biomedical and Behavioral Research. It was this commission that issued *The Belmont Report: Ethical Principles and Guidelines for the Protection of Human Subjects* (National Commission, 1979), which provides the ethical and philosophical template that frames research involving human subjects in the United States today. The report articulated three fundamental ethical principles for research involving human subjects:

- Respect for persons
- Beneficence
- Justice

For every social work researcher, the core values of the social work profession remain constant standards against which decisions are measured. The principles outlined in the Belmont Report are fully consonant with the NASW Code of Ethics and with other similar codes that govern the profession in other countries (e.g., Australian Association of Social Workers [AASW], 1999; Aotearoa New Zealand Association of Social Workers [ANZASW], 2007; British Association of Social Workers [BASW], 2002; International Federation of Social Workers [IFSW], 2004).

The value of respect for persons is associated with the principle of voluntary participation, which prohibits overt or covert coercion of individuals to participate in research. People have a right of refusal and can decline to participate, and in doing so they also have a right to know that this decision will have no repercussions. Informed consent requires that prospective participants are fully informed about the procedures and potential risks involved, and once apprised of these, they can choose to participate or not. The Code of Ethics (NASW, 1996, 2008, section 5.02), states that social work researchers must gain prior written consent from thoroughly informed research participants. Only when "rigorous and responsible review of the research" justifies its value, and "equally effective alternative procedures" including informed consent are not feasible is waiver of explicit consent ethical (2008, section 5.02g).

In addition, research participants have a right to confidentiality. In practice, this restriction often means that identifying information will not be made available to anyone who is not a direct research team member but will be available to all of those who are. A stricter standard of *anonymity* exists, wherein participants remain anonymous throughout the study; but this level of restriction can be difficult to sustain, for example, when participants have to be measured at multiple points in time.

The principle of beneficence requires you to ensure that you do not expose participants in your study to risk of physical or psychological harm. This is a more complex issue than it may appear initially. In child protection, for example, social workers do harm when removing a child from a parent. However, the parent may pose a risk of significant harm to a child. It is the risk–benefit ratio that is the determinant of whether a particular child removal is an ethical act. Risk–benefit ratios are often unclear in social work when the efficacy of many interventions is not well established and when extraneous factors are often beyond the reasonable control of the practitioner.

The general approach at the dissertation level, therefore, is to try to limit risk to no more than would be experienced in the normal course of living. If you believe that your study poses more risk than this standard, you should consult closely with your committee chair.

The principle of justice requires you to treat participants fairly—for example, to be mindful that participants allocated to a nonintervention group may be harmed by their failure to receive treatment. Even by random assignment, it is unethical to allocate participants to no service or no treatment control groups when they would be denied beneficial services, subjected to potentially harmful effects, or denied access to services to which they are historically entitled (Cook & Campbell, 1979; Rossi, Freeman, & Lipsey, 1999).

It is your responsibility to consider all of these principles, standards, and issues and how they relate to your dissertation. It is also your responsibility to check the requirements for submission to the body responsible for ensuring adherence to these principles, the institutional review board (IRB) of your university. Every institution receiving federal funds to conduct research is required to have a mechanism for ensuring the protection of research participants. These bodies are typically called institutional review boards but may also be known as the human subjects review committee, ethics review board, or the independent ethics committee. All investigators are required to gain advance approval from their IRB before embarking on research involving human subjects, whether or not the research is supported by federal funds. The approval process usually applies to pilot studies also, so it is important to gain early familiarity with both the requirements and the timetable of your local IRB. The process may seem daunting; however, it is worth noting that some research projects are exempt or may receive an expedited review, just as some studies (e.g., those involving children or vulnerable populations) may require a full review. Exempt studies include those that, while protecting confidentiality, are conducted as part of normal educational practice or use educational tests, survey, interview, or existing data. It is also worth noting that the added level of scrutiny applied to research proposals by institutional review boards often makes a contribution to the quality of the research.

The IRB may require that you take some short courses (often online) in human subjects protection, the Health Insurance Portability and Accountability Act (HIPAA), and ethics in research. It is wise to get all of these issues dealt with as early as you can so that your research is not delayed by awaiting IRB sign-off.

Further guidance on the ethical responsibilities of social work researchers is available from the National Statement on Research Integrity in Social Work (CSWE, 2007), which includes helpful standards on human subjects, mentor/trainee responsibility, conflict of interest and commitment, collaboration, and data management. The U.S. Department of Health and Human Services Office for Human Rights Protection (OHRP) is another useful resource.

TYPES OF STUDIES

Discussion of the range of methodological approaches available should begin with a review of the philosophical distinction that is often drawn between positivist and postpositivist (or interpretivist) social research.

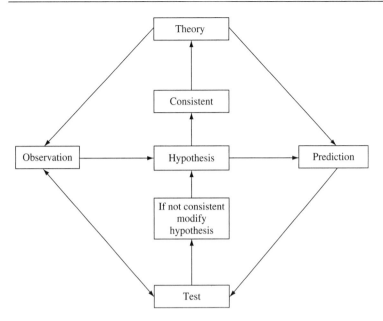

Figure 4.1 The deductive research cycle

The former is associated with quantitative approaches and the latter with qualitative approaches. Quantitative research in social work is based on the application of the scientific method to matters of interest to the profession. The scientific method (see Fig. 4.1) involves making observations, developing hypotheses, making predictions, and testing the predictions. If the predictions are borne out, this is seen as tentative support for the theory you are testing; if the predictions are not borne out, then the process starts again. As we shall see, there are challenges to conducting classical scientific experiments in social work research.

The scientific method depends upon the operationalization of variables of interest into numeric data, which can then be subject to statistical analysis. As you can see from Figure 4.1, quantitative research is primarily deductive, leading to theory testing. In addition, because of the way quantitative research is structured and the way samples are selected, the results of quantitative research are more likely to be reproducible and thus allow for generalizations. The capacity for others to conduct the same procedures in the same fashion and to replicate the results of previous studies is one of the hallmarks of the hard sciences, to which quantitative research owes its origins.

Qualitative social research is often seen as a reaction to positivist methods of social science. Instead of examining relationships in quantitative terms using statistical techniques, proponents of qualitative methods suggest that social research should provide depth and texture in understanding meaning. The concern is to understand people's lives as experienced by the person themselves, which implies making sense of life rather than testing universal theories or laws. As a consequence, this type of research is more closely related to the academic discipline of history than to natural science, seeking as it does to understand and interpret individual and collective meanings.

It is common to read criticism in the literature from qualitative researchers aimed at quantitative research, and vice versa. In our view, this is a false dichotomy. Applying the standards of one to the other is inappropriate and unnecessarily divisive. Each of these approaches functions within its own set of assumptions, deals with its own categories of questions, and has its own standards of rigor, and each can inform the other. The philosopher of science Thomas Kuhn concluded that "large amounts of qualitative work have usually been prerequisite to fruitful quantification in the physical sciences" (1961, p. 162).

Both qualitative and quantitative designs are required to be systematic. Indeed, systematization is a defining principle of research. The deductive nature of quantitative research stands in contrast to most qualitative research, however, which tends to be inductive. In other words, it generates rather than tests theory. Quantitative research moves from deductive theory to hypothesis, to observation, and finally, to confirmation, contrasted with the inductive observation, pattern recognition, tentative hypothesis, and ultimate theory formulation flow of qualitative research (see Fig. 4.2). Qualitative research often consists of describing participants' situations, meanings, and experiences using designs that are emergent and flexible in a fashion that is both fluid and nonlinear (Frankel & Devers, 2000).

When you select an approach for your dissertation it should be a reflection of what is required to address your research problem. You are likely moving toward a quantitative research design if you are

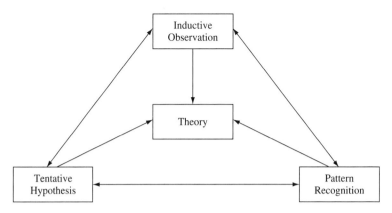

Figure 4.2 The inductive research cycle

asking questions of the type What? How much? How many? In what way? You are probably moving toward a qualitative design if you are asking questions of the type How? Why? Under what circumstances? Who are they? How do they? (see Fig. 4.3). You may also find that your choice is a reflection of your own personal values, as your values have likely helped frame your research interests in the first place.

QUANTITATIVE RESEARCH METHODS

There is an infinite array of quantitative research designs at your disposal, which is just as well because it can be difficult to do pure, experimental research in the messy and complex world of social work. Fortunately, a great many adaptations of true experiments have been developed. It is important that you consider these quasi-experimental and nonexperimental research designs and their applicability to your research problem before adopting any particular design. A complete and detailed description of each of the designs is well beyond the scope of this guidebook. However, we provide brief overviews of some of the more typical designs used in social work research as a potential guide to exploring these designs in greater detail elsewhere.

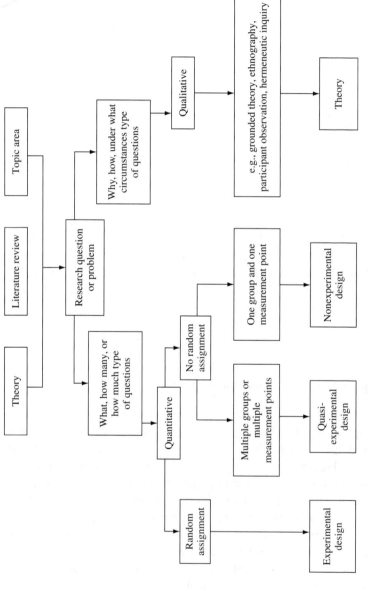

Figure 4.3 Simplified model of research design

Trochim and Land (1982) identify several issues that should be considered in the development of research. They suggest that design should

- Be grounded in theory.
- Reflect the settings of the investigation.
- Be feasible and sequenced.
- Include redundancy (e.g., use multiple measures and a large enough sample to accommodate attrition).
- Be efficient (i.e., should strike a balance between redundancy and feasibility).

Categorization of quantitative research designs may be done by randomization, number of groups, and number of waves of measurement (see Fig. 4.3). If the design includes random assignment, it is an experimental design; if it does not, it is quasi-experimental or nonexperimental. If the design involves more than one group, or more than one series of measurements, it is likely a quasi-experimental design (the Solomon 4 group design is an exception). If it contains no randomization, only one group, and only one point of measurement, it is a nonexperimental design (Trochim, 2006).

Methods of Control

One of the major features of your research design is the degree of confidence you can have that the research findings are directly attributable to your independent variable(s). In other words, you do not want to have one of your committee members suggest that your results are plausibly caused by some other factor. The best way to prevent this problem from arising is to ensure the most robust design that you can, given the constraints of the context in which you are working.

True experiments deal with the problem of alternative explanations for results by exposing the intervention group and a nonintervention (control) group to exactly the same factors except the intervention. Experimental research is based upon randomization—that is, random selection and random assignment—which means there is known probability across individuals in a population of any individual being selected for the study and equal probability of any individual selected being assigned to an experimental or control group. Randomization is the gold standard for ensuring comparability across groups; it minimizes the likelihood of initial average differences between the two groups. In other words, any statistically significant difference in the average value of outcomes for the intervention group and the control group is due to the impact of the intervention alone. Random controlled trials or true experiments are considered very robust models in relation to the threats to internal validity and external validity, which we discuss later in this chapter.

Cook and Campbell (1979) devised a notation for research design in which a randomized control trial would be represented thus:

$$R \quad O_1 \quad X \quad O_2$$
$$R \quad O_1 \quad \quad O_2$$

The notation above represents an explanatory design that uses hypothesis testing to uncover causal relationships between variables.

In this notation

R = randomized assignment to group,
X = exposure of a group to an experimental variable or event (the independent variable),
O = a measurement or observation of the dependent variable.

These notations are typically read from left to right to indicate the sequence of events. Vertical X's and O's occur at the same time. In the model above, it is clear that the participants are randomly assigned to each group, pre- and postintervention observations are taken of both groups, and only one group has been exposed to the experimental factor or intervention. A variation on this type of design may include a placebo group as well as the control and intervention groups. The notation for this design is below, where P represents the placebo.

$$R \quad O_1 \quad X \quad O_2$$
$$R \quad O_1 \quad \quad O_2$$
$$R \quad O_1 \quad P \quad O_2$$

The design above helps to control for findings that may be an artifact of participant awareness of the intervention rather than the intervention itself. The design allows for pre- and postintervention as well as within-group and between-group comparisons.

Disadvantages of Randomization

Cook and Campbell recognized that randomized control trials are not a panacea: "The case for random assignment has to be made on the grounds that it is better than the available alternative for inferring cause and not on the grounds that it is perfect for inferring cause" (1979, p. 342). Criticisms and difficulties associated with randomized control studies can be considered under several headings: policy utility, methodological, ethical/practical, and cost (Burtless & Orr, 1986).

Policy utility may also be described as the black box problem. A randomized control study can tell us that an intervention or program is or is not effective, but not necessarily why. There are also several methodological issues with randomized control trials, such as the Hawthorne effect wherein participants react to experimental conditions, not to the intervention itself. Practically, these types of designs are frequently unable to detect unintended consequences. In addition, they are demanding of potentially scarce resources—for example, people, money, and time. Limited resources are often a major concern for doctoral candidates who have their heart set on graduating before they reach an age at which they may be eligible for Social Security.

Earlier in this chapter we discussed the ethical issues associated with the random assignment of people to a nonintervention group, thus depriving them of important services. Despite their preeminence as the standard against which many other designs are measured, randomized control trials are not a panacea and are not the most commonly used design in social work research.

Nonexperimental Design

Nonexperimental methods, also referred to as natural experiments, are used when the independent variable is not under the control of the researcher or, in other words, is nonmanipulable (Shadish, Cook, & Campbell, 2002). This lack of experimental control may be because the independent variables have already occurred (e.g., social problems, disease processes, natural disasters, injuries, accidents) or when it would be unethical to manipulate the independent variable (e.g., child maltreatment, domestic violence). Exploratory studies of this type are most effective when using panel or cohort data, or through the use of matching techniques described below. The notation for this nonexperimental design is

$$X \quad O_1 \quad O_2 \quad O_3$$

In a panel design, the same people are observed or interviewed more than once. For example, children awaiting adoption may be interviewed while on the waiting list, then again after a match has been made, and then again when they have been placed with a family. Panel designs contrast with cohort studies, in which a group is studied over time but *different* members may be the individual study participants each time. For example, former users of substance abuse treatment programs may be surveyed at 3 months, 6 months, and 12 months after discharge, but the surveys may go to different members of each cohort for each time period.

Pre-experimental Design

The single group pre- and posttest design is a common means of estimating the impacts of interventions. Descriptive designs are not very robust because they are unable to account for alternative explanations of observed effects. Without a counterfactual (i.e., an alternative condition without the intervention), it is difficult to assess the intervention effects, but descriptive designs are an improvement over many exploratory designs because they collect pre- and postmeasures of the dependent variable.

Campbell and Stanley (1963) use the pre- and posttest design to illustrate the full range of factors that can undermine internal validity (confounds or threats) in quasi-experimental evaluation. If, when you draw up your research design, it looks like the notation below,

$$O_1 \quad X \quad O_2$$

you can make it more robust by adding groups, or observations, thus turning it into a quasi-experimental design. The notation of the single group design graphically illustrates the problem of having no counterfactual. You can see that though the group can be compared with itself, within-group comparison does not provide satisfactory control for potential confounds. To take an extreme example, if a group of foster care children were being assessed to determine the level of their physical development, the researcher might ask them to do a standing high jump against a wall at O_1 to see how high they can reach. Assuming that foster care is X, the intervention being evaluated, our intrepid researcher may perform the same test 1 year later at O_2. If the children can jump considerably higher at the second observation, measured by how high they can touch on the wall, how confident are we that any improvement in their ability is attributable to the foster care intervention? In other words, can the researcher rule out alternative explanations for the findings? The answer, of course, is no. The most plausible explanation is that the children are now 1 year older and bigger and physically more able, simply due to their increased age. Such a threat to internal validity is called maturation (processes that take place over time) and is just one of the potential threats that good design is intended to mitigate.

Quasi-experiments

Though not strictly true experiments, quasi-experiments are explanatory designs that can provide valid and reliable evidence about the relative effectiveness of an intervention compared with another intervention or no intervention. Quasi-experimental methods refer to those research designs that compare the outcomes of intervention and control groups by methods other than randomization (Cook & Campbell, 1979). Quasi-experimental methods are useful when you do not have the capacity to apply random assignment, or when doing so would be unethical.

The use of quasi-experiments is an attempt to ensure that the right conditions are available to allow you to infer a presumed causal relationship between independent and dependent variables. The conditions are these:

- The causal factor occurs before the observed effects.
- The causal factor co-varies with, or is related to, the observed effect.
- Alternative explanations for the observed effect have been ruled out. (Campbell & Stanley, 1963)

It is the last of these three that is often the most difficult to establish and where skill in research design is essential.

The nonequivalent comparison group is a more robust design than either nonexperimental or pre-experimental designs. It involves comparison between an intervention group and one that is similar to it, the counterfactual. Pre- and posttest data are collected for a comparison group and an intervention group at the same time. The notation below shows the absence of randomization; this absence introduces the designation *nonequivalent*, which means that the comparison group can be assigned in any number of ways, except randomly.

$$O_1 \quad X \quad O_2$$
$$O_1 \quad \quad O_2$$

The purpose of the comparison group is to provide greater confidence that outcomes are a function of the intervention. For example, psychiatric inpatients are involved in a 12-week series of group therapy sessions in addition to their normal treatment regimen. The patients have not been randomly assigned to the group, though pre- and postmeasures of symptom severity are taken from the intervention group and a nonintervention group. This nonequivalent design allows for both between-group and within-group comparison of symptom severity. The design, however, is susceptible to selection bias (where differences between groups are not randomly distributed between them), which can be mitigated or controlled for by the use of some type of matching.

Statistical Matching Designs

Statistical matching designs are similar to the pre- and post-nonequivalent control group method outlined above. In this type of design, the comparison group is so closely matched to the treatment group that the only difference between the two groups is the impact of the intervention.

In general, one-to-one statistical matching tends to perform better than matching at the group level. In other words, matching individuals with other individuals is more effective than matching groups with groups. For statistical matching to be successful, observations are required on variables statistically related to the dependent variable. In our psychiatric patient example, matching the intervention group members with the comparison group members might include diagnosis, gender, race, age, medication, treating physician, and physical health.

One of the drawbacks with matching is the almost inevitable realization that there is some other variable that should have been considered. In the example above it might be the number of prior hospitalizations.

Simple Time Series Design

The notation for the simple time series design is

$$O_1 \quad O_2 \quad O_3 \quad O_4 \quad O_5 \quad X \quad O_6 \quad O_7 \quad O_8 \quad O_9 \quad O_{10}$$

Each O represents an observation at a different point in time. These designs do not require a control or comparison group (though clearly the addition of one would enhance the design). In the notation above there are five preintervention observations, followed by the intervention represented by X, which in turn is followed by five more observations. In our psychiatric patient example, instead of having a comparison group, a time series design may involve measuring symptom severity each week for 5 weeks before the intervention period and 5 weeks following. Examination and statistical comparison of the pre- and postintervention slope can provide indications of the potential effect of the intervention.

Internal Validity

The many variations of research design are intended to maximize internal and external validity, which Campbell and Stanley (1963) defined as the basic requirements for an experiment to be interpretable. Internal validity addresses the question, Did the experiment and the experiment alone make a difference? External validity addresses the question of generalizability: To whom and to what contexts can we generalize these findings? The major threats to internal validity are these:

- *History* refers to the events occurring during the first, second, and or subsequent observations in addition to the experimental variables that may have had an impact on the experiment. As an illustration, if some of the foster children in our jumping example had been selected for track and field in their schools and had thus received special training in the standing high jump, their scores would likely have increased.

- *Maturation* refers to processes taking place within the participants through the passage of time—for example, growing older as in our foster care sample, or becoming hungrier, more tired, heavier, taller.

- *Instrumentation* refers to changes in a measurement tool or in the raters or observers, any one of which may produce changes in the measurements obtained. We will discuss the necessity for interrater reliability in the next chapter; suffice it to say that measurement instruments, whether they are rulers or surveys, should measure the same thing in the same way when used by multiple raters.

- *Testing* refers to the effects of taking a test upon the scores of a second testing. One of us recently had an experience in which the administrators of an agency, concerned about the effects of testing on worker knowledge of agency policy, did not want the workers to be pretested in case they learned the policy. Managing the threat thus impeded the overall goal of workers learning the material.

- *Statistical regression* operates when groups have been selected for intervention on the basis of their extreme scores. Galton (1886, p. 246) showed long ago that the principle of regression to the mean leads to the attenuation of extreme scores. In other words, the intervention did not make the difference. The change was simply due to extreme scores reverting to a more normal distribution, regression to the mean.

- *Selection bias* results from differential selection of respondents for the comparison groups. It relates to factors that may affect outcomes, for example, individual ability or previous history. Randomization does not mitigate selection bias by eliminating it but by distributing the possibility between groups. In quasi-experimental designs, statistical models can be used to mimic the selection processes by holding the selection processes constant.

- *Experimental mortality* is a potential threat to internal validity because intervention and comparison groups should be statistically equivalent when outcomes are measured, not just when group selection takes place. Participants may drop out between selection and observation in ways that are related to their group status and thus the processes of attrition may differ between groups.

External Validity

External validity refers to the degree to which "a causal relationship holds over variations in persons, settings, treatments, and outcomes" (Shadish, Cook, & Campbell, 2002, p. 21). In other words, external validity refers to whether the findings of research are generalizable. Campbell stressed the importance of external validity and referred to it as "situation specific wisdom," suggesting that without it, researchers will be "incompetent estimators of program impacts, turning out conclusions that are not only wrong, but are often wrong in socially destructive ways" (Campbell, 1984, p. 42). Some of the major threats to external validity include the following:

- *Representativeness* may arise when pilot or demonstration studies are conducted under conditions in which there are many resources in a supportive context. Positive findings for the study may not generalize to a less supported or less resource-rich context.
- *Reactivity* can occur in a study when participants are aware that they are involved in a research project and this causes them to behave in ways that affect the dependent variable.
- *Pretest-treatment* interaction occurs when pretesting sensitizes participants to aspects of the treatment and this sensitization has an influence on posttest scores.
- *Multiple treatment interference* occurs when participants receive more than one treatment and the effects of prior treatment interact with later treatments.

The most parsimonious way to control for threats to both internal and external validity is robust research design. Your design is the plan for your dissertation study; as such, it provides a picture of the controls you have established and hence the confidence you can have in your results. Typically in social work research, however, we are left with a compromise. Often programs or interventions under study are so unique that generalization is limited. In addition, resource and ethical issues place constraints on the level of control available. Ultimately you have to build the most robust design you can with a combination of front-end loaded (design) and back-end loaded (statistical) controls (see Chapter 6). It is relatively easy to conceptualize increasing control in quasi-experimental designs. Using the Cook and Campbell (1979) notation, you can add more groups or more observations to provide more opportunities for comparison. It is the capacity to make inferences about variation within and between groups that is central to explanatory, or hypothesis testing, research. In fact, there are really only four questions asked about the dependent variable. Did it go up? Did it go down? Did it stay the same? Was any change caused by the independent variable? It is the last of these questions that requires all of the opportunities for comparison.

QUALITATIVE RESEARCH METHODS

Social workers are generally effective in settings that require listening and questioning. Much of the focus of social work education at the undergraduate and graduate level emphasizes communication strategies. This emphasis on communication can lead to a higher degree of comfort with qualitative than quantitative research methods because they seem more familiar. Many times when candidates attend on-campus job interviews, however, they are unable to articulate the difference between their qualitative research and journalism. This is in part because they have not been encouraged to apply a high degree of rigor to their qualitative study. Shek, Tang, and Han (2005) evaluated the quality of qualitative social work research published from 1990 to 2003 and concluded that the quality was not high and that there was a general failure to pay enough attention to issues of study philosophy, auditability, bias, credibility, consistency, and data interpretation. A typical example is a researcher wishing to evaluate services at a homeless shelter for women and families and who interviews a number of residents, staff, and other stakeholders. The researcher then possesses a wealth of information with which he or she could write a social history of the shelter. Even so, without a defensible rationale for sample selection, application of a particular qualitative research methodology, coding of responses beyond content of the conversation, interpretation of results in relation to previous findings, reciprocal connection to theory, and validity, trustworthiness, and credibility checks this is not a rigorous piece of dissertation research. Stated differently, though much may have changed in the years since Shek and colleagues did their analysis, the major issue is that qualitative research needs to be as rigorous in its approach as any other type of research.

Notwithstanding these qualitative quality issues, in the United States there is an increasing trend toward qualitative research at the dissertation level and beyond. Shek, Lee, and Tam (2007) reported that up to December 2006 there were "621 and 1727 citations when the search terms 'quantitative' and 'qualitative' were used, respectively" (p. 821). In European social work, qualitative research at the dissertation level is even more prevalent than in the United States (Lyons, 2003).

When conducted with sufficient attention to academic rigor, qualitative research can be useful in allowing researchers to gain understanding of why, how, and under what conditions programs, policies, or interventions are or are not effective. Qualitative research has great utility when the research context is not sufficiently understood and when the perspectives of receivers of service are of interest as well as those of the deciders, planners, and implementers of services. In-depth analysis can provide helpful insights into the experience of intervention program recipients and this is particularly useful in the search for unintended consequences of intervention. In other words, qualitative research is typically descriptive or exploratory research.

Methods of Inquiry

Grounded Theory

The grounded theory approach to qualitative research consists of a set of steps intended to lead from data to the discovery or development of theory (Glaser & Strauss, 1967). Grounded theory is explicitly emergent; it does not seek to test hypotheses but rather to find what theory accounts for the research situation as it is. Grounded theory uses both inductive and deductive reasoning, the former in the process of generating theory from data and the latter in the process of constant comparison. The basic method of grounded theory is to read and reread a textual database and label variables, concepts, properties, and their interrelationships. Such open coding is the identification, naming, categorization, and description of phenomena found in the text. Each unit in the text— word, line, sentence, paragraph—is read in search of the answers to What is this about? What is being referred to here?

As data are coded, theoretical propositions are generated, categories are developed, patterns are detected, and working hypotheses are established. Through theoretical sampling, more cases are added and more observations and connections are made, which are then compared to the previously developed working hypotheses. Initially, new cases are added based on their similarity to earlier cases. When no new insights are forthcoming from the similar cases, the researcher harnesses dissimilar types of cases. This iterative process is repeated until no new insights are forthcoming. The overall cycle continues until the researcher is satisfied that further recruitment will not change the findings.

Ethnography

Adapted largely from the field of anthropology, ethnography is the study of a culture, group, or society and of the social rules, mores, patterns, and understandings upon which the study group is based. Ethnographic inquiry aims to elicit the cultural knowledge of a studied entity. In other words, ethnography seeks to examine what one needs to know to function as a competent member of a group. As is common in qualitative research, ethnography involves a naturalistic approach, avoiding manipulation of the group in any way. Ethnography shares with other types of naturalistic inquiry a desire to capture first-order meanings of participants and to relate these to second-order categories and constructs developed by the researcher. Ethnography allows the researchers to gain enough familiarity with a culture or society to understand it from the inside out (Chambers, 2000). In ethnography, the researcher becomes an observer of, and a part of, the system under study. For example, a social work researcher studying the culture of families in homeless shelters would spend time living in a shelter to be both part of and observer of that culture.

Participant Observation

Street Corner Society (Whyte, 1955), *Tally's Corner* (Liebow, 1967), *Asylums: Essays on the Social Situation of Mental Patients and Other Inmates* (Goffman, 1961), *The Presentation of Self in Everyday Life* (Goffman, 1959), *Behavior in public places: Notes on the social organization of gatherings* (Goffman, 1963a) and *Stigma: Notes on the management of spoiled identity* (Goffman, 1963b) represent some of the most important social research studies ever conducted. The three researchers, Whyte, Liebow, and Goffman, all engaged in participant observation, which is one of the most powerful ways to come to understand a group and their activities. Participant observation is a means to get as close as possible to a group without disturbing the natural operations of its members (Hammersley & Atkinson, 1995). Participant observation is differentiated from ethnography in that the extent of involvement can range from complete observational detachment to complete participative involvement, and anything in between (Gold, 1969). Regardless, in participant observation, the researchers remain detached from the research—that is, they are "objective observers."

Hermeneutics

In hermeneutic inquiry, researcher and participants work together to reach a shared understanding. This shared understanding is a structural element of hermeneutic study called the hermeneutic difference (Kelly, 1990). The hermeneutic rule of movement represents movement from the whole to the part and back to the whole again when analyzing conversational interactions with or between study participants. In hermeneutics there is an order presumed to facilitate the process of understanding; instead of collecting all interview data and then moving on to analysis, the first series of interviews is analyzed before proceeding with the next series of interviews. In the hermeneutic circle, feedback is provided to the participants about the researcher's understanding and then further discussion takes place. Through this iterative process of dialogue, analysis, feedback, and subsequent dialogue, shared understandings are reached between the researcher and participants. In common with most types of naturalistic inquiry, these steps are not mutually exclusive and may not occur in a strict linear sequence.

The process begins with the understanding of the researcher—that is, what the researcher believes about the group, context, or issue—and continues with the examination of all interview texts, seeking an expression that reflects the essence of the text as a whole. Understanding of the whole is the starting point for analysis because the meaning of the whole influences understanding of the parts of the text.

Every sentence or section is investigated to uncover its meaning in relation to the subject matter, thus facilitating the identification of themes. As in grounded theory this insight leads to in-depth understanding of the phenomenon studied. Each sentence or section is then related to the meaning of the whole text. Passages are then identified that are thought to be representative of the mutual understanding between the researcher and the participants (Kelly, 1990).

Threats to Credibility

Reliability and validity are crucial to quantitative research, and though couched in somewhat different terminology (e.g., credibility, trustworthiness, defensibility, and generalizability), these issues are equally important in qualitative research. Both types of research must be systematic. Systematization is demonstrable and evident in high-quality research whether inductive or deductive. Below, we return to some of the methods of ensuring rigor in qualitative research that we touched upon in the previous chapter.

Triangulation

Robust research designs frequently include some type of triangulation, bringing together different types of data, different data sources, or different ways of looking at data to the research endeavor. Triangulation can be used to verify data as well as to enhance understanding of the data. Denzin (1989) describes four types of triangulation: methodological triangulation, data triangulation, investigator triangulation, and theory triangulation.

- *Methodological triangulation* may consist of "within method" triangulation, in which a range of different lines of questioning is used to approach the same issue, and "between method" triangulation, in which different data collection methods are combined. Data from all sources are then reviewed for consistency.
- *Data triangulation* consists of combining data from more than one source. For example, a researcher studying a nonprofit multiservice agency may solicit data from a cross section of stakeholders, from board members to service users. The researcher may also collect data at different periods and from different sectors of the organization (e.g., foster care, counseling, adoption, or substance abuse treatment units in the same organization).
- *Investigator triangulation* is similar to the consensus method discussed in Chapter 3. It involves more than one researcher examining the data and often approaching them from completely different angles.

- *Theory triangulation* involves the use of different theoretical positions to explore the compatibility of these different theories with the data. In addition, theory triangulation involves looking at the data from different assumptions to see how different initial assumptions might affect interpretation.

Validation

The concept of validation is closely related to triangulation and consists of member validation or member checks. In other words, research participants determine whether the researcher's interpretation of meaning and events accords with their own. The method is used to check on bias and the quality of research. Peer or expert validation involves sharing findings with others who have expertise in the research phenomenon or the population. Research can also be validated through corroboration with other research on the same or similar phenomena, or with the same population. The determination of credibility in a qualitative study is largely a function of the process by which the data were collected. As a result, in a qualitative dissertation, it is necessary to take great pains in detailing how the researcher went about collecting, handling, analyzing, and interpreting the data.

MIXED METHODS RESEARCH

So far, we have presented qualitative and quantitative research as separate entities; in many instances, however, both approaches are used in the same project. Mixed methods research involves adopting a research strategy employing more than one type of research method, which may include a mix of qualitative and quantitative methods, a mix of quantitative methods, or a mix of qualitative methods. Mixed methods research can also mean working with different types of data, or working in different research paradigms (Bryman 2001, 2006).

Mixed methods allow for several ways to combine results from different data analyses. These include

- *Corroboration:* Data from one method confirms findings from the other.
- *Elaboration:* Qualitative data may expand upon or elaborate quantitative findings.

- *Initiation:* Use of one method stimulates new questions or hypotheses to be tested by the other.
- *Complementarity:* The two types of data are juxtaposed, which may allow a larger and more detailed understanding of the phenomena under examination.
- *Contradiction:* Findings from one method contradict the other, but when explored further, greater insight into the problem at issue may be developed. (Bryman, 2001, 2006; Hammersley, 1996; Morgan, 1996; Rossman & Wilson, 1994)

Mixed methods research may therefore involve combining qualitative and quantitative approaches in a single study. It has been suggested that epistemological, ontological, and methodological differences between the two make it difficult if not impossible to conduct mixed methods research (Sciarra, 1999). On the other hand, there are those who believe that such approaches are not only possible but both desirable and in frequent use (Greene, Benjamin, & Goodyear, 2001; Ponterotto & Grieger, 1999).

By now, you will have gained a sense of the level of complexity inherent in both qualitative and quantitative approaches to research and some sense of the difficulty of learning and applying both methods in a single dissertation. However, one of the areas of social research that most commonly uses mixed methods approaches is program evaluation, a favorite topic of dissertation study in social work.

PROGRAM EVALUATION

Rubin and Babbie (1997) identify three purposes for program evaluation:

- Evaluating program outcome and efficiency
- Evaluating program implementation problems
- Evaluating for program planning and development

They also distinguish summative from formative evaluation. Summative (impact) evaluation is associated with evaluating program efficacy, effectiveness, and efficiency. The aim is often to provide estimates of the effects of a program or service in terms of what its impact was expected to be at program inauguration, or compared with some other intervention, or with doing nothing.

Formative evaluation, also called process evaluation, asks how, why, and under what conditions a program or service works. The structures, mechanisms, and processes that determine success are evaluated in formative evaluation. The distinction between summative and formative evaluation is not always clear. Often program evaluation is based on the development of a program logic model (see Fig. 4.4) that contains both summative and formative elements to be measured as well as quantitative and qualitative elements (see, e.g., Doueck, Bronson, & Levine, 1992).

Program evaluation as a dissertation study also has an added sociopolitical dimension because there are now potentially more people with a vested interest in your research. Agency administrators, staff, service users, and other stakeholders may all be affected by the process and outcome of your dissertation study.

POLICY EVALUATION

Much like program evaluation, policy evaluation benefits from the use of a variety of analytical tools and methodological procedures, including many of those detailed in this chapter (quantitative and qualitative methods, experimental and nonexperimental designs, descriptive and experiential methods, etc.). As with all research projects, the precise strategy and methods used in a policy dissertation should be driven by the research question being addressed.

Again, in a comparable fashion to program evaluation, the determination of the impact of a social policy involves asking questions about whether the policy has achieved its goals, whether it has worked, and if so, for whom and under what conditions. Thus, policy evaluation requires the use of both summative (measure of effectiveness) and formative (reasons for effectiveness) evaluation. Social policies often spawn what have been described as unintended, or unanticipated, consequences (Merton 1936). Although these outcomes may be beneficial, they may not be completely benign. For example, a decision by a state child protective services (CPS) agency to divert children from foster care to community alternatives may have the intention of reducing

Program Logic Model

Agency: Dissertation Example
Program: Home Visitation

Version Date: April 01, 2009

Inputs	Activities	Outputs	Outcomes		
			Initial	Intermediate	Long term
MSW level supervisor. Para-professional home visitors. Supervision and support for home visitors and families.	Home visitation for higher risk new families, focusing on (1) Positive parent-child interaction, (2) Healthy child development, (3) Stronger family functioning, and (4) Appropriate community linkages.	Increased knowledge of child development. Increased awareness of supportive community resources. Number of home visits. Number of community linkages made. Number and type of educational materials disseminated.	Improved parent-child interaction. Improved family functioning. Reduced family stress.	Reduction in risk of child maltreatment. Reduction in no. and % of referrals to CPS. Reduction in no. and % of substantiated cases of child maltreatment. Target reduction = 100% of families should experience no substantiated maltreatment.	Increased safety, permanence, and well-being for children.

CPS = child protective services.

Figure 4.4 Sample program logic model

disruption in the children's lives, but it may have the unintended consequence of exposing them to greater risk of maltreatment. A quantitative study may provide helpful information on the number of children affected, and a qualitative approach may help the researcher understand if there were other unintended consequences. In other words, policy evaluation can make use of the range of research technologies available to address social research questions.

SUMMARY

In thinking about your research design, it is helpful to think in terms of the questions that your dissertation is intended to answer. Whether your study is ultimately qualitative, quantitative or a combination, there are methods available to structure your study that provide the degree of rigor required at the dissertation level and that also allow you to demonstrate your skill in their adaptation.

ACTION STEPS CHECKLIST

☐ Learn how the IRB process works at your institution.
☐ Take any training required by the IRB.
☐ Discuss any potential ethical issues with your dissertation supervisor.
☐ Maintain and uphold social work values and the highest ethical standards at all stages of your dissertation research.
☐ Write down the criteria that you will use to inform your decision about selecting a research methodology.
☐ Identify the major qualitative and quantitative studies in your area of interest. Identify how they differ, not just in terms of their approach but also in terms of the questions they address and the insights they achieve.
☐ Determine whether the corpus of research on your topic is explanatory, exploratory, or descriptive.
☐ Determine what types of questions your research is intended to answer.
☐ Identify the research methodology most appropriate for answering your research question.

☐ Identify the methods you will use to control for confounding explanations and threats to internal and external validity, or

☐ Identify your methods for controlling threats to credibility and trustworthiness, as well as for ensuring defensibility and generalizability.

☐ Check for congruence throughout design, data management, and writing of results.

5

Sampling and Measurement

He uses statistics as a drunken man uses lamp-posts—
for support rather than illumination.

Andrew Lang (1844–1912)

In their review of dissertation quality, Adams and White (1994) identified small sample size as a common problem in social work dissertations. Size is just one issue in sampling, however; it is not simply the number of subjects that is significant, but also who they are, and how, where, and when they were selected. How can the researcher be sure that the sample truly represents the population? What methods are available to help determine how many participants should be selected for any given study? What is a confidence level and how does it relate to a confidence interval? In this chapter we will discuss these and other questions about sample size and selection.

Doctoral research frequently involves the measurement of abstract concepts. For example, a student may be interested in exploring the relative vulnerability of elderly nursing home patients in two different establishments, or with differing levels of family support. All too often, in the early stages of conceptualization the issue of measuring the concepts of interest—in this case, vulnerability and family support—is taken too lightly. How is vulnerability defined and operationalized? How is family support defined and operationalized? How will they be measured? How will we know if the instrument used really measures vulnerability, for example, and not some related phenomenon (e.g., frailty)? How do we know that the instrument will measure vulnerability in the same way when used by different raters? How do we know that the instrument will measure vulnerability in the same way with different groups? These questions and many more are connected to the measurement properties of instruments that all too often loom late in the thinking processes of novice researchers.

Chapter 5 will provide general guidelines for identifying, selecting, and describing a study sample as well as issues to consider when identifying, selecting, and developing appropriate measures.

OBJECTIVES

By the end of this chapter you will be able to

- Design a sampling strategy.
- Choose measurement instrumentation appropriate to your dissertation.

TOPICS

- Sample design
- Statistical power
- Effect size
- Sampling in quantitative research
- Sampling in qualitative research
- Measurement
- Issues in measurement with human measures

In this chapter, we will discuss sample selection in quantitative and qualitative research, as well as statistical power, effect size, and issues in measurement.

SAMPLE DESIGN

In quantitative research, sample design is a process that answers two basic questions:

- How are units for the sample to be selected?
- How many units are going to be selected?

The first question is concerned with inclusion and exclusion criteria, representativeness, and generalizability. The second question is associated with the level of confidence you may have that your sample is large enough to detect any experimental effects, while also being small enough to be manageable. Before exploring these questions further, we should clarify a number of terms associated with sampling.

Sampling Unit

Units are the individual entities that make up the sample. They might be cells, cases, individuals, groups, families, organizations, or com-munities—indeed, any type of entity that forms the basis of a study. One of the important issues to resolve in your dissertation sampling plan is the *unit of analysis.* In a study measuring family adaptability, for example, is the unit of analysis the individual family members or the family as a whole? In a study measuring the acquisition of social skills among students who participate in a special course offered in a local high school, is the unit of analysis the individual student, the class, the grade level, or the entire high school? When measuring community cohesion, is the unit of analysis the neighborhood, the families in the neighborhood, or the individuals who live there? Such questions are of critical importance because they raise issues of inde-pendence of data and the power of the study to determine differences if they exist.

Sample

A *sample* is a specified number of units selected from a population. The main reason for selecting a sample rather than studying an entire population is somewhat obvious; by studying a representative sample, the researcher is able to draw conclusions about the overall population in a more cost-effective and efficient manner. Stated differently, a sample is studied to draw valid conclusions about the larger group without the need to study every unit in that group. Thus, your sample will be selected for study because the total population is often too large to study given limited time and resources. The sample should therefore be representative of the population from which it is drawn. As we shall see below, this is often best achieved by random sampling.

Sampling Frame

A *sampling frame* includes the list of potential units from which a specified number are drawn. The frame is typically some type of list including all, or at least most, of the units in the study population. For a researcher planning a national study of NASW members, a comprehensive NASW membership list would be ideal as the sampling frame from which to draw the sample. The sampling frame approximates the population and, depending on the population under study, may be a close or distant approximation. The NASW membership list (a nonstigmatized group) is likely a closer approximation of that actual population than would be a statewide list of domestic violence victims, the homeless, substance abusers, the mentally ill, or any other stigmatized population because of difficulties in knowing the true extent of any stigmatized group.

Representativeness

Representativeness is achieved when the sample provides an accurate reflection of the characteristics of the total population. Therefore, before collecting your sample, you should adequately and carefully define the population, including the members to be included, and then be sure that the sample adequately represents that population. The population for a study of admission to foster care might be all children admitted in a state during a particular year, and the systematic random sample might be every tenth child admitted. The representativeness of the sample indicates how much confidence you can have in generalizing from the sample to the population.

Sampling Error

Typically, researchers talk about two major types of error in sampling. *Random error* is the natural propensity of a sample to differ from the population from which it was drawn. *Nonrandom error* or sampling bias occurs when there is systematic distortion of a sample. For example, drawing a sample from the population of parents of gay, lesbian, bisexual, transgendered and queer (GLBTQ) youth from those parents who are members of parent support groups or particular church groups may be problematic. Leaving out parents who do not belong to these groups establishes a systematic distortion and would erode the representativeness of the sample.

Confidence Level and Confidence Intervals

Using the concepts of *confidence level* and *confidence intervals*, it is possible to make sampling error estimates. For example, it is common to read of polls in which the authors report a specific confidence level with a margin of error within a specific range (e.g., 95% degree of confidence that candidate A has a 50% approval rating with a margin of error of plus or minus 5 percentage points). The confidence level is the probability value $(1 - \text{alpha} = 1 - \alpha)$ associated with a confidence interval. It is typically expressed as a percentage. For example, if $\alpha = 0.05 = 5\%$, then the confidence level is equal to $1 - 0.05$, which equals 0.95—in other words, a 95% confidence level.

Suppose an opinion poll predicted that in an election today the Democratic Party would win 55% of the vote. A 95% confidence level plus or minus 3% would mean that the pollster believes there is a 95% likelihood the Democratic Party would get between 52% $(55\% - 3\%)$ and 58% $(55\% + 3\%)$ of the total votes cast.

A *confidence interval* thus provides us with a range of values likely to include a population parameter that is unknown. The estimated range may be calculated from a given set of sample data. If we take independent samples repeatedly from the same population and calculate confidence intervals for each independent sample, then a certain percentage (i.e., the confidence level) of the intervals will include the unknown population parameter. Confidence intervals, as we shall see later, are also very useful in the context of determining the impact or effect of an intervention. Their usefulness arises because they can provide more information than a hypothesis test, which is either supported or rejected, whereas confidence intervals give a range of values for unknown parameters.

Confidence is thus written in terms of how far away from the true estimate the sample estimate might be. With larger samples there is no absolute guarantee that you will match the population value, but there is a smaller probability of being a long way off. The tradeoff, however, is in how many sampling units (people, cases, families, etc.) study resources can accommodate. Sample design is about reducing the chances of getting a nonrepresentative sample while also minimizing the resource demands of your research. It is a balancing act.

Determining Sample Size

A number of factors must be determined to establish the appropriate or optimal sample size.

Statistical Power

Statistical power considerations are crucial to the adequate design of a quantitative research project (Cohen, 1969). Without sufficient statistical power your conclusions may be of little use. An effective method of determining sample size is the use of statistical power analysis. In a companion text in this series, Patrick Datallo (2008) uses a 4:1 ratio of β (the probability of Type II error) to a (significance level) such that if you set the alpha level at 0.05 you can determine power by computing

$$1 - 4(0.05) = 0.80.$$

The concept of statistical power is a function of

- Significance level α or the probability of a Type I error. For example, $\alpha = .05$.
- Power to detect an effect. This is expressed as power $= 1 - \beta$, where β is the probability of a Type II error. For example, as above, $\beta = .80$.
- Effect size, (d) knowing that the smaller the effect, the more difficult it will be to find.
- The standard deviation (σ, for the population and, s for the sample) of the hypothesized effect size.

- Sample size. A larger sample size generally leads to parameter estimates with smaller variances, giving you a greater ability to detect a significant difference.

Knowing any four out of the five components of statistical power, that is alpha, beta, effect size, and standard deviation, automatically determines the fifth. Typically, we are hoping to determine the sample size (n) given the values of the other four (α, β, d, σ).

There is logic to the use of power analysis in a quantitative dissertation. Why complete a study with a sample too small to detect variability? Unfortunately, lack of power is a common problem. The Type II error rate resulting from underpowered studies (i.e., where the sample size was too small) in psychology and education is estimated to be 50% or more (Lipsey & Wilson 1993; Sedlmeier & Gigerenzer, 1989). You would not wish your dissertation to be underpowered, but neither would you want too large a sample. The first problem may negate your findings; the second may overwhelm your resources.

In conducting experimental and quasi-experimental research the aim is to falsify the null hypothesis that the intervention has no effect. In other words, the purpose is to refute the notion that any observed differences between the intervention and comparison groups result from sampling error. *False positives* or *Type I errors* arise when we mistakenly believe that sampling error differences between intervention and control groups are a result of the intervention. A statistical significance of 95% is really a *Type I* error rate of 5%, meaning that there is a 5% chance of failing to reject a *true* null hypothesis. In a hypothesis test a *Type I* error occurs when the null hypothesis is wrongly rejected.

The corollary is a *false negative* or *Type II* error where statistical power of 80% means a 20% chance of failing to reject the null hypothesis when it is *false* and a real statistically significant impact exists. Statistical power can be thought of as the probability of detecting a statistically significant difference when a real effect exists. Typically, the probability of a *Type II* error is unknown. If the null hypothesis is not rejected, it may still be false (a *Type II* error) if the sample was not large enough to detect differences. For any given set of data, *Type I* and *Type II* errors are inversely related; in other words, the smaller the risk of one, the higher the risk of the other.

The probability of a *Type II* error is generally unknown but is represented by β (beta) and written thus:

P (Type II error) = β

The power of a statistical hypothesis test measures the test's ability to reject the null hypothesis when it is actually false—that is, to make a correct decision. In other words, the power of a hypothesis test is the probability of not committing a *Type II* error, or of detecting an effect if the effect exists (Cohen, 1969). Mathematically, we obtain this probability by subtracting the probability of a *Type II* error from 1:

Power = 1 − P (type II error) = (1 − β),

where P = probability and β is the probability of making a *Type II* error. Therefore, the maximum power a test can have is 1, and the minimum is 0.

In a study examining the effectiveness of an intervention, the null hypothesis suggests that the intervention is no better, on average, than no intervention or a comparison intervention. A *Type I* error would occur if we concluded that the two groups scored differently on postintervention measures when really there was no difference between them. A *Type II* error would occur if we concluded that the groups scored the same on posttest measures, suggesting that there was no difference between intervention and nonintervention, or comparison groups when there really was a difference. It is in the conservative nature of the scientific tradition that *Type I* errors are considered more problematic than *Type II* errors. Hence, researchers err on the side of caution and use the aforementioned 4:1 ratio for the *Type I* to *Type II* error, although you should consider the consequences of each type of error in your particular circumstances.

Effect Size

Cohen suggested that "the primary product of a research inquiry is one of measures of effect size, not *p* values" (1969, p. 12). Effect size allows us to ask different questions from those asked in hypothesis testing. The latter answers the question, Does it work? The former answers the question, How effective is it in a range of contexts?

You may determine the effect size for your dissertation in several different ways. First, the large and growing number of meta-analyses available provides a rich source of information that allows you to review a great many studies with effect sizes measured in a common metric (e.g., Cohen's d, or r^2). Second, you may use your knowledge of the topic area to make an estimate of whether you believe you will get a small, medium, or large effect. Cohen (1969) somewhat hesitantly defined effect sizes (using d to represent effect size) as "small, $d = .2$," "medium, $d = .5$," and "large, $d = .8$," stating that "there is a certain risk inherent in offering conventional operational definitions for those terms for use in power analysis in as diverse a field of inquiry as behavioral science" (p. 25). Even small effects, however, may be practically important or clinically significant.

$$\text{Effect size} = \frac{(\text{Mean of intervention group}) - (\text{Mean of comparison group})}{\text{Standard Deviation}}$$

or

$$d = \frac{m_1 - m_2}{\sigma}$$

The standard deviation or σ (sigma) is a measure of the spread of a set of values. In the equation above, it refers to the standard deviation of the population from which the different treatment groups were taken; this standard deviation is not usually known, but it can be estimated from the standard deviation of the control group (Glass, 1976), or preferably from a pooled value from both the control group and the intervention group (Cohen, 1969; Rosnow & Rosenthal, 1996). The pooled standard deviation is the square root of the average of the squared standard deviations for each group. If the variances of the two groups are equal, then the standard deviation of either group can be used (Cohen, 1969).

As you can see from the above equation, another advantage of effect size over tests of statistical significance is that effect size is independent of the sample size. Effect sizes are expressed in standardized units that allow for comparison across studies, which is why they are so important in meta-analysis.

Imagine a study had an intervention group whose postintervention score on a 50-point scale was 30. For the nonintervention group, the postintervention score on the same measure was 22. If the two groups were the same size and the pooled standard deviation was 10, the calculation of Cohen's d for this study would look like this:

$$d = \frac{30 - 22}{10} = \frac{8}{10} = 0.8$$

The standardized effect size or $d = 0.8$. What this represents is the difference between the two means standardized by using their standard deviation. An effect size of 0.8 indicates that four-fifths of a standard deviation separates the two means. If the effect size represents a positive difference, then this denotes improvement (if higher scale scores are equated with improvement). Deterioration would be represented by a negative difference. For an excellent summary of various effect size measures and their interpretation, see LeCroy and Krysik (2007). Though beyond the scope of this chapter, there are also available methods to determine if the magnitude of variance introduced by the intervention is clinically significant (Jacobson & Truax, 1991; Ogles, Lambert, & Masters, 1996).

Having determined α, β, d, and σ, we now have all of the components required to determine the required sample size. In Datallo's companion text in this series (2008) he recommends using GPower (Erdfelder, Faul, & Buchner, 1996), a free power analysis program available at http://www.psycho.uni-duesseldorf.de/aap/projects/gpower/. In addition, there are numerous programs available on the Web or as add-ons to existing statistical packages. Datallo also provides a helpful resource list of free and commercial programs as well as information about add-on packages to statistical software (e.g., SAS, SPSS).

SAMPLING

Having determined how many units or participants you will need in your sample, it is also important to determine how you will select them. Researchers distinguish between two broad types of sampling: probability and nonprobability sampling. The major difference between these two is that probability sampling involves random selection and nonprobability sampling does not. This does not necessarily mean that nonprobability samples are unrepresentative of the population; it does mean that nonprobability samples are not supportable by recourse to probability theory. Probabilistic samples, as we saw above in the discussion about confidence levels and confidence intervals, allow for the determination of the probability that your sample represents the population. Probabilistic samples are thus more likely to be representative (Cochran, 1977).

Probability Sampling

Probability sampling allows calculation of the probability of an element being selected. Probability theory gives us rules that help decision making in sample selection. First, if we select numerous independent random samples from a population, the sample statistics we get will be predictably distributed around the population parameters. We can also calculate an estimate of how closely the sample statistics cluster around the true value (Rubin & Babbie, 2007).

In short, your sample should be scientifically chosen so that each person in the population has a measurable chance or known probability of selection. You can then generalize from your sample to the larger population with known levels of precision.

To avoid systematic error, sampling should be designed to guard against unplanned selectiveness. For your dissertation, therefore, you need to develop a replicable or repeatable sampling plan that allows for the random selection of a sample capable of meeting the goals of your study. To answer the question about how units for your study should be selected, think about your research question and think about what would be the sample with the greatest likelihood of providing answers. You can also refer to your review of the literature and examine how others addressing similar questions selected their samples. What was their unit of analysis? What were the inclusion and exclusion criteria? As you review the literature you will see that there are many methods of sample selection, several of which are presented below.

Simple Random Sampling

Simple random sampling is a bit like pulling numbers from a hat, but if your population is large you may need a very big hat. However, just using luck of the draw may not provide you with a good representation of any subgroups in your sample. In using simple random sampling to select participants for a study of a violence prevention program in high schools, you may by chance underrepresent a particular racial group. This underrepresentation would be a sampling error due to normal variation, but it would raise potential problems of representativeness. To avoid this type of sampling error, researchers often adopt a stratified sampling plan.

Stratified Sampling

Stratification is the act of dividing your sampling frame into strata or groups before sampling. Using the violence prevention program example, you might take a sampling frame of schools and then sort them into size strata before sampling. The sample would then be described as a sample stratified by size. If a list of the students was available that recorded age, race, and gender, then it would be possible to divide the list into age, race, and gender strata before sampling. This sampling method involves dividing the population into subgroups based on variables known about those subgroups, and then taking a simple random sample of each subgroup.

Stratified sampling may be either proportionate or disproportionate. In a proportionate stratified sample the sampling frame is divided into strata, but the same sampling proportion or fraction is applied to each stratum. Each stratum is thus sampled from its correct proportion. In a disproportionate stratified sample, the sampling proportion differs between strata. In other words, individuals from those strata with the highest sampling fractions will be overrepresented in the sample. Disproportionate sampling is useful when there is a need to increase some group's representation within a particular stratum or strata. The Council on Accreditation (COA), for example, requires that accredited agencies oversample high-risk cases in their case quality auditing procedures (COA, 2006). This practice ensures that the signal importance of these cases is reflected in the final audit sample.

The main advantage of stratified sampling over simple random sampling is the increased confidence that the sample drawn matches the sampling frame. If the sampling frame in our violence prevention program is stratified by age, race, and gender and a proportionate sample is selected, then the sample will match the sampling frame in the distribution of all three. In other words, the age, race, gender distribution is controlled. If the study results are correlated with age, race, and gender, then by stratifying the sample you have reduced the risk of nonrepresentativeness. Stratification thus reduces standard errors.

Cluster Sampling

A clustered sample is selected in two or more hierarchical stages, different units being selected at each stage, and with multiple subunits being selected within higher order units. Again using the violence prevention program as an example, you would take a sample of students selected by first sampling schools and then selecting students within schools. This is a two-stage clustered sample, the clustering based upon students within schools.

If you wished to conduct a household survey of experiences of childhood maltreatment, you could select a random sample of zip codes, then a random sample of households within those zip codes; then individuals might be selected within households. In this design, adults are clustered within households (assuming more than one adult is selected per household) and households are clustered within zip codes. The more the total sample is spread across clusters, the lower is the chance of taking an extreme sample and the lower is the standard error.

Multistage Sampling

In this sampling strategy you would combine simpler sampling methods to address sampling needs in the most effective way possible. For example, the violence prevention researcher might begin with a cluster sample of all schools in a school district, then set up a stratified sampling process within clusters. Within schools, the researcher could conduct a simple random sample of classes or grades.

Nonprobability Sampling

Nonprobability sampling methods can be divided into accidental or purposive models. In nonprobability sampling where the sampling frame is not well defined the chance that an individual unit will be selected is unknown. Mall intercept samples (i.e., samples drawn from volunteers recruited at shopping malls) represent a common example of bability sampling. The haphazard method of sample selection is that the distribution of sample statistics is also unknown.

Convenience Sampling

In convenience sampling the researcher makes little or no attempt to ensure the representativeness of the sample. Samples are selected because they are accessible. College students are a favorite group for psychological research, for example. Convenience samples can provide useful information, particularly in pilot studies, but generalizing from this sampling method is fraught with difficulty.

Purposive Sampling

As its name implies, purposive sampling is done with a purpose in mind. Typically researchers have one or more specific predefined groups whom they are seeking. Ads seen in newspapers seeking participants with a particular health problem—"Wanted: Men and women over 30 years of age who are experiencing difficulties in sleeping"—would be an example of a purposive sampling.

Snowball Sampling

A form of purposive sampling, snowball sampling participants are typically selected by using existing study participants to recruit among people they know. A study of people living on the street might adopt a snowball sampling strategy as the most parsimonious and effective way to recruit participants. Studies of other hidden populations or those difficult to access such as drug users, commercial sex workers, and street gangs often adopt snowball sampling. In this approach, participants are not selected from a sampling frame and thus samples are subject to numerous biases. However, for some types of research, snowball sampling is the only way to develop a meaningful cadre of participants.

Quota Sampling

Quota sampling makes use of stratification principles but allows for substitution. For example, a researcher may know that the population of interest is 35% Hispanic, 20% African American, and 4 Selection would then take place until the sample makeup m population. If people refuse to participate, then others are selected to nll their place, but only in the same proportions. Absence of random selection means that quota sampling does not necessarily provide representative data.

SAMPLING IN QUALITATIVE RESEARCH

Sample design and selection in qualitative research does not follow the same logic as probability sampling for quantitative research, but it should still be systematic and logically defensible. The nature of a qualitative sample and the rationale for its selection, just as with quantitative research, should be spelled out in the context of study objectives. The researcher must actively seek out and include participants who can challenge preliminary theories. Clearly, differences in study philosophy will also lead to different sampling decisions. Researchers must therefore align their sample and sampling methods with their selected research paradigm. For example, research on the phenomenological experiences of a group can be conducted with samples of different sizes and compositions. Ethnographic and participant-observation research provide fewer opportunities to select the sample a priori and demand more capitalizing on opportunities that arise during fieldwork. Even so, there remains a requirement for rational and defensible decisions that arise from the research question.

As we saw above, in purposive sampling, selection criteria are described in the early stages of sample design. Decisions may be based in the review of the literature or on the study questions. Purposive sampling strategies may also be used in qualitative research where they are designed to enhance the researcher's understandings of individuals or group experience and to lead to the development of theory. Miles and Huberman (1994, p. 34) suggest that the following types of cases are likely to be the most information rich:

- Typical cases that represent normality for the study sample
- Deviant cases that represent unusual or extreme manifestations of the phenomenon of interest

- Negative cases that are exceptions to general rules that provide disconfirming manifestations of the phenomenon of interest

In qualitative research, it is extremely important to pay attention to the complexity of cases when developing a sampling frame. In doing so, consideration should be given to how many sites or participants can realistically be managed in a qualitative study. Recruiting participants and then not giving their potential contribution the time and energy that it merits is a waste of the participants' time and borders on unethical behavior.

In contrast to purposive sampling, theoretical sampling decisions are made during the study on the basis of emergent theory rather than prior to the study's commencement (Gilgun, 1994; Glaser & Strauss, 1967; Strauss & Corbin, 1990). The process is iterative and generally associated with grounded theory. Indeed, the process is integrated with and imitative of grounded theory research design:

- An initial sample is selected
- The data are analyzed.
- Emergent theory is developed.
- A further sample is selected to help refine an aspect of the emerging theory.
- The data are analyzed again.
- There is further development of theory.
- More cases are selected.

This process continues until data saturation is reached. In the context of theory development, which is often the purpose of qualitative research, theoretical sampling is particularly useful. The intention in qualitative sampling is not to provide a precise representation of the population but to select a diverse enough sample to generate insight (Gilgun, 1994; Glaser & Strauss, 1967; Strauss & Corbin, 1990).

In terms of how many units or elements should be in the sample, qualitative research logic again differs from that of quantitative research. Statistical power is not the driving factor. Samples must be big enough to include key subgroups and to reflect diversity, but that is all. Representativeness is moot as far as this type of study is concerned.

Large samples may indeed be a hindrance and would almost certainly be unmanageable given the level of intensity of interaction with participants or other data sources. The richness of qualitative studies is in the depth of data collection and analysis rather than in the breadth, and thus, the appropriate size of a sample is often a matter for continued judgment throughout the research process. Particular attention should be paid toward the end of fieldwork, however, so that any gaps in information can be filled.

The primary research instrument in almost all qualitative research approaches is the researcher. This means that these approaches require the researcher to establish, maintain, and terminate relationships with participants. Absent the social skills and motivation to develop and sustain relationships with study participants, researchers would find it very difficult to recruit and maintain a study sample.

MEASUREMENT

As we have seen, quantitative research requires the operationalization of dependent and independent variables in order to test hypotheses. Hypothesis testing answers the questions: Did things go up? Did things go down? Did they remain the same? To measure whether things changed or remained the same, research requires effective instrumentation. Natural science research often uses instrumentation that measures height, weight, length, size, distance, temperature, color, position, energy, and so forth. Though social science research typically measures less tangible or straightforward concepts—for example, skills, attitudes, feelings, relationships, symptoms, and behaviors—the instrumentation required to measure change in these variables demands the same reliability and validity of measurement as those in the natural sciences. Although not a perfect analogy, the example of the simple tape measure is often helpful. A tape measure must yield the same results when used by different people (interrater reliability) and when used at different times (stability or test/retest reliability). Different tape measures must yield the same results when measuring the same distance (construct validity). Each unit on a tape measure must be exactly the same as every other comparable subunit (internal consistency). When a tape measure tells us that an object is 1 foot long, we need to have confidence that the object is indeed 1 foot long. Tape measures therefore must be accurate (validity). Just as tape measures must demonstrate reliability and validity, so should measures in social science research.

Reliability

Reliability is the extent to which an instrument yields the same results on repeated trials. Validity is the extent to which an instrument yields accurate results. Hence, without reliability there can be no validity. Reliability, though a necessary condition, is not a sufficient condition.

Interrater Reliability

Just as with our tape measure example above, interrater, or interobserver reliability is the extent to which two or more observers, coders, or raters using the same measurement instrument agree on their results. If three MSW level child protective services (CPS) workers use the same risk-assessment instrument to measure the level of risk posed by the same family, and one reports findings of high risk, one medium risk, and one low risk, there would be a clear problem in consistency. The risk-assessment instrument would appear to have low interrater reliability. Although training, education, and skill development can improve interrater reliability, this is only true if the measurement instrument is inherently consistent. In order to evaluate interrater reliability, researchers most commonly use the correlation coefficient. Observers may not agree on the exact score every time, but their scores may vary in the same direction each time, yielding a high level of correlation (e.g., $r = .80$).

Test/Retest Reliability

Stability reliability or test/retest reliability is the agreement of measuring instruments over time. In conducting research, if your measures reveal different scores over time you need to have a degree of confidence that these changes are not due to a level of temporal instability in your measurement instrument. To determine stability, a measure or test is repeated on the same subjects at two different times. If the score correlation between the two tests is above 0.7, then the instrument is deemed to have acceptable test/retest reliability. Some precautions need to be taken, for example, to ensure that test conditions are identical for both test and retest and that tests are far enough apart that participants in the retest do not recall their answers on the previous test.

Internal Consistency

When you have an instrument with multiple items, each of which is scored and then combined with scores from the other items to give a total score, internal consistency is an important consideration. Internal consistency is the extent to which tests or procedures assess the same characteristic, skill, or quality. In the same way that you could fold a tape measure in two and the two halves would each be the same length, it is possible to compare the two halves of a social science measurement instrument and then assess the correlation between the total scores on the two halves. The most common statistic for calculating internal consistency is *coefficient alpha,* which can be calculated using most statistical software packages and is the average of all split-half correlations.

Validity

Validity refers to the degree to which a study accurately reflects or assesses the specific concept that the researcher is attempting to measure. While reliability is concerned with the stability and consistency of the actual measuring instrument or procedure, validity is concerned with the instrument's ability to reflect the concept that the researchers set out to measure. Just as there are multiple types of reliability, there are multiple forms of validity. In fact, it would be more accurate to speak of the reliabilities and validities of an instrument than its reliability and validity.

Face Validity

Face validity is concerned with how accurate a measure or procedure appears. Indeed, it might be argued that face validity is not really a true form of validity. It is as simple as using one's judgment to make a decision about whether an instrument appears "on the face of it" to measure what it should. To use an extreme example, if a judge in the Olympic javelin competition tried to measure the distance thrown by using a bathroom scale, we could reasonably conclude that the measurement instrument did not have face validity. However, an instrument designed to measure self-esteem may measure some other related phenomenon, such as self-efficacy, which may be similar and even connected, but not the same. Making an assessment based on face validity alone, where concepts are complex, overlapping, or related, has great potential for mistakes.

Content Validity

Content validity is based on the degree to which a measurement reflects the intended domain. Carmines and Zeller (1991) use the example of a measure to determine mathematical ability. They point out that a measure addressing only addition would not have content validity because the domain of mathematical ability also includes the capacity to do division, subtraction, and multiplication. Like face validity, though, content validity is based on judgment rather than empiricism.

Criterion-related Validity

Criterion-related validity, sometimes called instrumental validity, is an assessment of the accuracy of a measure taken by comparing it with another measure previously demonstrated to be valid. Checking the length of a meter on our tape measure by ensuring that it is actually equal to the distance that light travels in a vacuum during a time interval of 1/299,792,458 of a second (the definition of a meter) (*Conférence Générale des Poids et Mesures* [CGPM], 1983) is a difficult though accurate way of determining the criterion-related validity of our tape measure. Holding our tape measure against another tape measure would be a simpler alternative for checking its criterion-related validity.

There are two subtypes of criterion-related validity: concurrent and predictive validity. In concurrent validity one might develop an instrument to assess risk of acquiring a sexually transmitted disease (STD). The instrument could be tested against a number of study participants divided between those who have already contracted an STD and those who have not. With the researchers blind to the participants' condition, an assessment of the instrument's capacity to correctly classify into known groups is an assessment of concurrent validity.

Predictive validity is the capacity of an instrument to predict criteria that will be known in the future. Imagine that the STD risk instrument is administered to study participants at time 1 and predictions made about the presumed level of risk for contracting an STD. If the participants are followed up for a specified period to determine their actual status at time 2, this is an assessment of predictive validity. In this example we have the capacity to predict who is likely to contract an STD and to evaluate the veracity of the prediction. Concurrent validity is sometimes confused with predictive validity. Just because the instrument referred to above can differentiate those individuals with STD from those who do not have STD does not mean that the instrument would be able to predict with reasonable accuracy who is at risk for getting an STD.

Construct Validity

Construct validity represents the level of agreement between a measure and a theoretical concept. For example, if you developed a measure of global job satisfaction you might expect that it is related to the way you have theoretically conceptualized the phenomenon. You might expect that it is related to workers' desire to change jobs (turnover intent). If your theoretical construct suggests that as satisfaction goes down turnover intent goes up and this is borne out by your results, then this represents a degree of construct validity.

Construct validity can also be broken down into two further sub-categories: convergent validity and discriminant validity. Convergent validity is the general agreement among ratings, gathered independently of one another, where measures should be theoretically related. If your measure of job satisfaction correlates with those people identified by supervisors as having lower or higher job satisfaction, then it can be said to have convergent validity.

Discriminant validity is the lack of a relationship among measures that theoretically should not be related. Using the job satisfaction example, you would want your scale to be closely correlated with theoretically similar constructs but not closely correlated with those that are dissimilar. For example, if your global job satisfaction scale were highly correlated with measures of depression or IQ, then it would not have good discriminant validity, being unable to discriminate job satisfaction from depression or IQ (except if depression and IQ are in fact related to job satisfaction).

In relation to the selection of measures for your dissertation, we suggest that you select validated measures with known psychometric properties where they exist, unless you are specifically developing measures as the major topic of your dissertation. In either event we recommend that you examine texts such as Fischer and Corcoran (2007), and Web sites such as the Buros Institute of Mental Measurements (http://www.unl.edu/buros) for guidance to validated measures and associated issues.

ISSUES IN MEASUREMENT WITH HUMAN MEASURES

Some qualitative researchers eschew the whole notion of applying positivist concepts of reliability and validity to qualitative research (Stenbacka, 2001). Others suggest that reliability and validity should be considered in study design, data analysis, and judgment of rigor (see Lincoln & Guba, 1985; Patton, 2002). Still others have recommended that the quality of a study should be judged by paradigm-specific criteria (Healy & Perry, 2000). Table 5.1 contains the concepts recommended by Lincoln and Guba (1985) as criteria for examining the consistency of qualitative research and the equivalent quantitative criteria.

Lincoln and Guba (1985) also recommend the use of inquiry audits to enhance the dependability (reliability) of qualitative research. These audits can be used to examine both the process and the product of the research for consistency (Hoepfl, 1997).

The use of triangulation in qualitative research is, as we have seen in earlier chapters, a common way to enhance the rigor of the process. Triangulation may include the use of investigator, method, and data triangulations to record the construction of reality (Johnson, 1997; Padgett, 1998). An open-ended qualitative perspective such as that of grounded theory is fully consonant with data triangulation by allowing

Table 5.1 Criteria for Judging Rigor of Research Methodology

Quantitative research	Qualitative research
Internal validity	Credibility
External validity	Applicability or transferability
Reliability	Consistency or dependability
Objectivity	Confirmability or neutrality

participants in research to assist the researcher in the research question as well as with the data collection. Engaging multiple methods, such as observation, interviews, and recordings, will lead to more valid, reliable, and diverse construction of realities. Triangulation may include multiple methods of data collection and data analysis, but it does not suggest a fixed method for all researchers.

In summary, whether you are engaged in quantitative or qualitative research the choice of sampling strategy is crucial to the success of your research. Decisions about sampling will determine to a large extent your capacity to answer your research question. Too large a sample is wasteful of resources; too small a sample calls into question the power of your research to detect effects. Similarly, judicious choices about measures, whether they are paper and pencil or human, require a degree of attention to issues of reliability and validity, or credibility, dependability, and neutrality.

ACTION STEPS CHECKLIST

- ☐ Define the unit of analysis.
- ☐ Define the population.
- ☐ Develop your sampling strategy.
- ☐ Determine required sample size.
- ☐ Ensure sufficient statistical power.
- ☐ Select valid and reliable measures, or
- ☐ Define steps to ensure credibility and trustworthiness in qualitative research.

6

Data Management and Analysis

Statistics means never having to say you're certain.

Anonymous

In Chapter 6 we will examine some issues related to the analysis of quantitative and qualitative data. In addition, we will present the application of social research methods and statistics to social problems and social work research.

Both quantitative and qualitative methods are integral components of social work research. The hallmark of quantitative research is the ability of the researcher to obtain relatively large amounts of quantitative data, often on large samples, through a systematic process of instrument development, application of standardized measurement procedures, data collection, data processing, and data analysis. Qualitative analysis on the other hand is more of an iterative set of processes that allows the researcher to collect vast amounts of in-depth information or data on a smaller sample. In qualitative research, data collection and data analysis may occur concurrently. The different processes involved in qualitative analysis can also overlap in time and are reciprocally complementary.

OBJECTIVES

By the end of this chapter you will be able to

- Develop plans for the management and analysis of both quantitative and qualitative data.

TOPICS

- Quantitative data
  - o Management
  - o Collection
  - o Preparation
  - o Analysis
- Qualitative data
  - o Management
  - o Collection
  - o Preparation
  - o Analysis

QUANTITATIVE DATA

As with every other step in the dissertation process, data management is driven by the research question. In previous chapters, we have examined how to develop directional hypotheses and how to identify and specify dependent, independent, moderating, and mediating variables. We have looked at the development of a sampling plan and learned what to look for in measurement instruments. In this chapter, we examine the development of a data management plan, which for our purposes includes identifying the data to be collected, identifying how it will be collected, ensuring data protection, preparing the data for analysis, and finally, analyzing the data. The presentation of results from your analysis is presented in Chapter 7.

DATA MANAGEMENT

Data management is concerned with the sequence of steps that lead from data collection to data analysis and includes the following:

- Data collection: gathering data from the various data sources
- Data logging: ensuring that details of data receipt and data source are recorded
- Data protection: ensuring that data are stored in a secure manner compliant with HIPAA regulations, internal review board requirements, and ethical protections required by the NASW code of ethics
- Data preparation: cleaning, checking, sorting, transforming, recoding, and combining the data as appropriate
- Data analysis: running the relevant descriptive and inferential data analytic tests required by your research question, and/or ensuring credibility and trustworthiness of qualitative data analysis

The principal of equifinality means that there are many different ways to approach the tasks above, and a number of tools are available to help structure each step. Among the tools you may find useful in your data management are these:

- Data collection plan, which specifies what data will be collected in what form by whom, when, and where it will be collected, how questions about data collection are to be resolved, and how the data will be conveyed to data storage, logged, cleaned, recoded, and analyzed
- Logic model, which describes the inputs, activities, outputs, and outcomes of your research (see Chapter 4 for an example of a logic model)
- Data log, which records what data have been received, entered, cleaned, checked for accuracy, and ultimately how you got from the raw data to the analyzed data. The log will eventually include details of combined variables, data recodes, themes identified, and data transformations that may have taken place.
- Data collection instruments, which include coding abstraction sheets as well as various other measures used

- Data dictionary or code book, which includes specification of vai, ables as they are operationalized in your study, variable names, and possible responses. Ultimately, the data log and data dictionary may form the basis of a technical summary of your research
- Data analysis plan, which describes the steps to be taken to move from raw data to results

Data Collection

A critical feature of data collection is the development of a data collection plan. There are several steps in creating such a plan, most of which we have already discussed. First is the determination of what you are going to measure (dependent and independent variables). Second is the identification of the sources of the data (e.g., sample, subsample, secondary data sets). Third requires the determination of operational definitions of variables of interest and the development, adoption, or adaptation of measures with sound psychometric properties to collect relevant, accurate, and useful data. The logic model may be a useful component of the data collection plan because it helps structure thinking about the flow of events of interest and their interconnections.

Data Logging

The endpoint of the data collection component of data management is the logging or recording of data as they arrive. Depending on the type of study you are conducting, data may be based on direct observations that are systematically coded and recorded, mail or electronic surveys, case-records review, interviews, review of secondary data sets, or self-report scales, to name a few. Data may come in slowly in small batches over which you have great control or may arrive in volume in a manner more difficult to manage. In whatever form data arrive, we recommend keeping a careful record or log of what has been received and from where. There are many choices about how to log your data, ranging from pen and paper to database systems (e.g., Microsoft Excel or Access, Apple Numbers, Claris Filemaker, Open Source spreadsheet) or statistical packages (e.g., SPSS, SAS, STATA). Provided you have an up-to-date record of what data you have and have not yet received, the mechanism is largely a matter of choice, expertise, and availability of resources.

As soon as data are received, they should be checked to see if they are accurate. Doing this early in the data logging process gives you the potential to go back to original sources for clarification. You should check for complete, accurate, legible responses, look for missing data, check for outliers, and examine the data distribution for normality.

Of coure this process may be more difficult to organize if you are part of a research team or have others collecting the data for you, but we believe that it is important to ensure data integrity as soon as possible.

The Inter-university Consortium for Political and Social Research (ICPSR, 2005) makes a number of recommendations for data preparation. The ICPSR recommendations are specific to archiving data for later use, but many of the principles are suitable for logging dissertation data. These recommendations include developing a structure that contains the following information:

- Name of principal investigator(s) and affiliation at the time of data collection
- Official title of the data collection
- Funding sources; grant number and related acknowledgments
- Data collector/producer. Persons or organizations responsible for data collection, and the date and location of data production
- Project description
- Sample and sampling procedures
- Date, geographic location of data collection, and time period covered
- Data source(s)
- Unit(s) of analysis/observation

The ICPSR also recommends maintaining a complete list of all variables, their full names and corresponding abbreviations, with each potential value for each variable recorded, including missing values and for every variable, its name, description, format, date collected, and which instrument was used to collect it (sometimes referred to as a code book). Maintaining such a list from the start of the study may not seem especially relevant, but once you are weeks, months, perhaps years removed from the original data collection, this information can become essential in recreating what you have accomplished and in identifying what else you might be able to examine in the data.

Data Storage and Protection

A good data management plan will ensure that original records (e.g., field notes, coded observation checklists, returned surveys, pre- and posttest instruments) are retained for an appropriate period of time. The National Institutes of Health and the National Science Foundation along with all federal government agencies and federally funded research projects require that grant recipients keep all data for 3 years after the final expenditure report of the grant has been submitted. The rules can be seen at the Health and Human Services Web site http://www.hhs.gov/ohrp/.

Each university also has its own policies and procedures for data storage and it is important to be cognizant of those that pertain to your institution. Often journals or professional organizations have their own requirements. For example, the American Psychological Association requires data to be maintained for 5 years after publication of the findings.

Typically, university IRBs require researchers to undergo HIPAA compliance training before receiving IRB approval to conduct a study. Satisfying the requirements of the training is one aspect; putting the requirements into effect is another. Details of HIPAA rules and standards can be viewed at the Web site http://www.hhs.gov/ocr/hipaa/.

As a researcher you are responsible for ensuring both the privacy of your study participants and the confidentiality of their personal information. Just as you document everything else in the research process, the safeguards that you establish should also be documented. It might be useful to think in terms of data security as a series of design choices (policy) with data protection thought of as a series of mechanisms (e.g., strong password protection, firewalls, tiered access, etc.) (Wulf et al., 1974).

It is important that unintentional breaches of data security are avoided by ensuring that all paper-based data are stored in locked, steel file cabinets or their equivalent, and that electronic data are also kept in the virtual world version of a locked, steel cabinet, with appropriate limitations on access, firewall protection, and appropriate encryption. It is also important that identifers are removed and stored separately from the data. Given the requirement to retain data, it is also important to ensure sustainable longevity for these arrangements. Your institution will have very clear minimum requirements for data storage and protection. In order to receive IRB approval you will have to provide details of your arrangements for the storage and protection of your data.

Data Preparation

Data preparation includes cleaning, checking, sorting, transforming, recoding, and combining the data as appropriate. The precise steps to be taken are a function of the nature of the study and the nature and sources of the data. The ICPSR guidelines are also useful when thinking about data preparation. They recommend, for example, that for each variable the following information should be made available.

The question. Record the exact wording of the question or the exact meaning of the datum. When your data collection is fresh in your mind, the cryptic note that you have left for yourself that "V7 = child age" may seem clear, but at some later point when you are trying to determine if this is the age of the youngest child, the oldest child, a particular child, or if this is child age at time of testing, of data entry, or of a specific incident, you may regret having left only a cryptic note.

Universe of information. Lack of specificity of the information universe can be problematic. If family counseling participants are asked to rate their coping and functioning on a 10-point scale, for example, it might be crucial to know if all family members were asked the question, if only parents were asked, if only one score per family was recorded or multiple scores representing each family member, or if a combined average was reported.

Missing data codes. It is inevitable that you will have some missing data. How you handle these missing data elements is important to your analysis. Make sure that you record what codes you have assigned to what types of missing data. For example, if an item was missed by the respondent it might be coded "99," but if the response was "not applicable," then you may use "88." Whatever convention is adopted, the codes must fall outside the range of valid values. Each statistical package handles missing data differently and there are different choices about how to handle missing data within each package, so you should check with the software that you are using. Useful resources when considering how to handle missing data are provided by Acock (1997), Allison (2001), Little and Rubin (1987, 2002), Jones (1996), and Shafer and Graham (2002). Shafer and Graham distinguish between types of missing data:

- *Missing not at random* (MNAR) where data related to both the dependent and the independent variable are missing. This type of missing data must be addressed because it represents a pattern that may have a significant impact upon results.
- *Missing at random* (MAR) where data related to the independent but not the dependent variable are missing
- *Missing completely at random* (MCAR) where data are missing but with no discernible relationship to either the independent or dependent variables

Shafer and Graham (2002) also describe different methods of dealing with missing data. These include

- *Listwise deletion*, which is useful when few data are missing, but erodes sample size and thus statistical power
- *Ipsative mean imputation*, which is useful when dealing with missing items from a scale, but may produce biased results
- *Maximum likelihood estimation*, which is useful for missing completely at random (MCAR) and missing at random (MAR) data
- *Multiple imputation techniques,* in which the average of multiple estimates of missing values is used

If you have significant missing data we recommend that you consult a reference source such as those cited above, and your committee chair, or statistical consultant.

Constructed variables and recode logic. We recommend that you provide an audit trail of the steps involved in creating any recoded variables. At the simplest level, this may be recoding continuous age data into age bands (e.g., 0–9, 10–19, 20–29, etc.). When analyzing data, you may well combine or recode variables to replace or substitute for existing variables. For example, if you have 10 separate variables that correspond to a 10-item measure, then you may combine these scores by adding them to create a value for the scale score. It is also important at this stage to record details of any reverse scored items. This type of item is often included in measurement instruments to mitigate response set bias. Before analyzing data it is important that reverse scored items are scored in line with other items in the same scale. Such alignment can be accomplished by the simple expedient of subtracting the actual item score (b) from the maximum possible score (a) and then adding 1, that is,

$$(a - b) + 1$$

For example, on a 5-point Likert-type scale where items ranged from 1 = "Strongly Disagree" to 5 = "Strongly Agree," a reverse scored response of "4 = Agree" would be recoded thus:

$$(a - b) + 1$$
$$= (5 - 4) + 1 = 2$$

In a statistical package this type of change is a simple recode procedure, but we cannot emphasize enough the importance of recording exactly what you have done, and how.

We have described in earlier chapters the necessity of keeping an audit trail for qualitative data, but the development of a similar audit trail is also important in the data logging and preparation stages of quantitative data management.

One of the consequences of recoding, combining, and transforming data is that it is difficult to keep track of the changes you have made. One way to keep track of any changes is to save new changes into a different version of your data set. In other words, do not discard or overwrite the old one (ICPSR, 2005). Version 1 may therefore be the one created at the end of the data collection process. Version 2 may be the one that you have after data cleaning. Version 3 may be the one after composite variable construction, and so forth. Keeping track of your data in this fashion will make it easier to track what you did and when. In addition, as with all important computer files, it is sensible to keep backup copies of your data.

Data collection instruments. Also ensure that you retain and store copies of all data collection instruments.

Coding instrument. Rules and definitions used for coding your data should also be recorded in case you need to refer to them later in the process.

Data transformations. Among the first tests that you will perform on your data are simple descriptive and distribution analyses to determine missing data and data outliers; you will also plot your data to check for normality of distribution. Many common statistical tests are based upon assumptions about the data (e.g., normality of distribution, independence of observations, homogeneity of variance), and violations of these assumptions can negate the power or efficacy of specific tests. Although some tests (e.g., *t*-tests) are known to be fairly robust in the face of violations of assumptions—that is, they do not lose much of their statistical power—others are not so robust (e.g., linear regression analysis) (Cohen, Cohen, West, & Aiken, 2003). Parametric tests require an assumption of normally distributed data, for example, but there are numerous data transformations that can accommodate violations of these assumptions and still maintain the integrity of your statistical analysis. When you plot your data, if it appears to approximate a normal distribution you probably do not need to make further accommodations. If your data appear skewed—that is, asymmetric (not in the form of a bell-shaped curve)—one of the data transformations (e.g., logarithm, square root, reciprocal) will likely give you what you need to make the data symmetric.

Whatever recodes or transformations you do make, it is vitally important that you keep a detailed record of what you did. One way to do this is to make copies of printouts indicating how data were recoded and keep them in a binder. The principle upon which these requirements are based is that it should be possible to work backward from your results through the data analysis, the various recodes and data transformations, to the original measures, and of course for other, later researchers to work forward from your data collection to conclusions.

DATA ANALYSIS

Once you have collected, cleaned, logged, recoded, and transformed your data as appropriate, you are ready to begin the first part of your data analysis: running summary measures, or descriptive statistics. Data analysis is often divided into the two major components of descriptive and inferential analysis.

Descriptive Statistics

One of the tasks in the data analysis stage is to take the material that you have entered into a data structure, which consists of rows and columns of data in raw form, and turn it into meaningful summaries that show relationships within the data. Reporting the number of years of education of a group of social workers simply by listing them will give your reader a vague sense of the range of scores, but summarizing the scores using a measure of their center (mean, median, mode) and a measure of their spread (range, or variance) is much more helpful. In describing your sample you may also test whether your intervention and non-intervention groups differ appreciably in any way on demographic measures (e.g., race, gender, socioeconomic status, education). Describing the scores for each group and whether any differences identified may plausibly account for differences in the dependent variable is an important step in data analysis. To do this you would choose *t*-tests—for example, when looking at whether men or women scored differently on a continuous measure of job satisfaction. For the same continuous dependent variable, you may run an analysis of variance (ANOVA) to examine the means for more than two groups—by race, for example. To determine the probability of a participant being an agency supervisor by race or gender, you may wish to run a chi-square analysis.

Inferential Statistics

Inferential data analysis involves exploring and determining relationships between variables (or subgroups). Did your intervention make a difference? Are the recipients of the cognitive-behavioral intervention now more able to cope in their everyday lives? Were the groups different? Did the gang members score higher on scales of aggression than young offenders who were not gang members?

Many doctoral students struggle when choosing the appropriate statistical tests with which to examine research questions. Although it is beyond the scope of this book to provide detailed guidance on every possible statistical test, it is possible to guide you through some basic questions. The answers to these basic questions will in turn help you in seeking advice from your statistical consultant, whether that is a person, a book, or the Web.

The types of statistical tests you choose are based upon your study question and the design you have chosen to test it. When testing your hypotheses, it is important to remind yourself what your research question is.

- Are you testing a hypothesis? If so,
  - Are you comparing two or more groups? If so,
  - How many groups are involved?
  - Are they paired (matched) in some way?
- Are you trying to quantify the association between variables or to predict outcomes?
- Are you trying to determine time to an event?
- What type of dependent or outcome variable is being assessed? Is it
  - Nominal?
  - Ordinal?
  - Interval?
  - Ratio?
- What type of distribution does your dependent variable have? Is it
  - Normal?
  - Binomial?
  - Skewed?

How many independent and dependent variables are involved? For example, linear regression compares one continuous dependent variable and one continuous independent variable. Multiple regression compares two or more continuous independent variables against one continuous dependent variable.

Motulsky (1995) has provided a helpful guide to choosing statistical tests in which he suggests that it is important to know when to choose parametric over nonparametric tests, one- or two-sided p values, and when to choose paired tests.

Parametric or Nonparametric Tests

We have already discussed the importance of determining whether your data are normally distributed. One of the reasons for making this determination is in the differences between parametric and nonparametric statistical tests. Parametric tests require continuous variables that follow a normal distribution, and nonparametric tests do not. Of course, in social research the assumptions around normal distributions and independence of data are rarely met. Consequently, there is a view that because nonparametric statistics are very robust and almost as powerful as parametric statistics one should not make a choice but rather run both. If no differences are found with a nonparametric test, the likelihood is that no differences will be found with a parametric test (Motulsky, 1995). Commonly used parametric tests are the t-test, Pearson's correlation, multiple regression, and analysis of variance (ANOVA); commonly used nonparametric tests include chi-square and Fischer's exact test.

One- or Two-Sided p Value?

Another decision you must reach before you run your analysis is whether to adopt a one-sided or two-sided p value. A p value is calculated for the null hypothesis that the two population means are equal, and any difference between the two sample means is due to chance. If the null hypothesis is true, the *one-sided p* value is the probability that two sample means would differ *in the direction* specified by the hypothesis just by chance, even though the means of the overall populations are actually equal. The two-sided p value also includes the probability that the sample means would differ that much in the *opposite direction*. A one-sided p value is appropriate when you are confident beforehand there either will be no difference between the means or that the difference will be in the direction you specify. If in doubt, Motulsky suggests you should select a two-sided p value (1995). Even so, though "riskier," a one-sided p value is a more powerful test.

Paired Tests

When comparing two groups, you need to decide whether a paired or an unpaired test is required. For three or more groups the term *repeated measures* is used, rather than paired test. Unpaired tests are used to compare groups when the individual values are not matched with one another. Paired, or repeated measures, tests are used when values represent repeated measurements on one subject (e.g., before and after an intervention) or measurements on matched subjects.

You should select a paired test when values in one group are more closely correlated with a specific value rather than random values in the other group. It is appropriate to select a paired test only when the subjects were matched or paired before the data were collected, however. It is not appropriate to base the pairing on data during the data analysis (Motulsky, 1995).

If you can answer or make a decision regarding all the above, then you are in a good position to determine the most appropriate statistical tests for your questions and data. There are many algorithm-type tools on the Web to help you with this decision making, for example, the one at UCLA at http://www.ats.ucla.edu/stat/mult_pkg/whatstat/choosestat.html, which we have found very helpful. You can use this or similar sources once you have defined what type of data you have and what type of analysis you would like to conduct. Consulting this UCLA site or others can help you determine the exact test required. One of the advantages of the UCLA site is that it gives hyperlinks to instructions on how to perform each test in SPSS, SAS, and Stata.

Another excellent resource is provided by John C. Pezulla, a retired faculty member in the Departments of Pharmacology and Biostatistics at Georgetown University. The site at http://statpages.org/ is very extensive and contains a huge list of free software for statistical analysis, including help in determining which test to use. You will also find links to many other resources at the Oxford University Press companion Web site.

QUALITATIVE DATA MANAGEMENT

As in quantitative research, data management in qualitative research is driven by the research question. The need for consistency of research philosophy and methodology, the need to clearly identify your data analysis methods and coding procedures, the need to ensure their consistency with your study philosophy and objectives have all been stressed. We have also looked at the special requirements of sampling in qualitative research as well as issues associated with humans as measures. It is now appropriate to examine the management of qualitative data, which, as is the case with quantitative research, is the collection, protection, preparation, and analysis of your data. Qualitative analysis, rather than referring to inferential statistics, involves the mutually contingent and nonlinear steps of data labeling, reduction, coding, summarizing, and interpreting.

Previously we have discussed the iterative nature of qualitative research and the multiple complementary and sometimes competing approaches to the process. This multiplicity of approaches is also reflected in data analysis. One of the more familiar data analysis techniques in qualitative research comes from grounded theory with its multistage coding procedures and steps of theory development described in Chapter 4 of this book (see Gilgun, 1994; Glaser, 1992; Glaser & Strauss, 1967; Strauss & Corbin, 1990). There are other data analysis methodologies associated with narrative analysis (Mishler, 1986; Riessman, 1993), discourse analysis (Blommaert, 2005; Carter, 1997; Gee, 2005; Labov, 1972, 1982; Nye, 1998a, 1998b; Schiffren, Tannen, & Hamilton, 2001; Sherman, 1994), ethnography (Goldstein, 1994; Hammersly & Atkinson, 1989; Van Maanen, 1988, 1995), descriptive and hermeneutic phenomenology (Cohen & Omery, 1994; Giorgi, 1985), feminist critical studies (Cosgrove & McHugh, 2000; Davis, 1994), and so forth. We have chosen to review analytic methods that apply more generally to most forms of qualitative research because of the plethora of models available.

Data Collection

Regardless of the philosophical or methodological approach, data must be collected and rendered amenable to analysis. In contrast to the strictly numeric data derived from quantitative research, data in qualitative research are words, albeit words in combination with other words. Data analysis involves the scrutiny, synthesis, and interpretation of these word combinations. The words may be derived from interviews, focus groups, textual materials, audio, video, observations, poems, or narrative. They may be based on pictures, paintings, sculptures, or other works of art, but ultimately the data are words that are intended to reflect the totality of an experience in context. Consequently, the researcher must provide both descriptions of events and contextual interpretations of these events.

The border between description and interpretation is often a very fine and permeable line in qualitative studies and it is thus important to convey clearly to the reader what is description and what is interpretation. Taylor and Bogdan (1998) provide guidance for writing field notes including guidance on the development of conventions for differentiating description from interpretation.

In the introduction to this chapter, we contrasted the discrete stages of quantitative research with the simultaneous processes of qualitative research. The sequential nature of the former means that note-taking and ultimately writing each stage of research is easily focused on a discrete element of the process. The nonsequential nature of qualitative research makes this a little more challenging, but one way in which qualitative researchers manage this simultaneity is to record contemporaneous field notes in different types or categories. The following four categories, for example, may be helpful in maintaining the boundaries between the simultaneous, parallel processes (Strauss & Corbin, 1990).

- *Field notes* (FN) provide a contemporaneous log of what happened. They may be based on live observation, audio, or videotaped material.
- *Personal notes* (PN) describe your reactions, feelings, biases, impressions, and preconceptions. These notes are helpful because you can use them later to examine your influences on the data collection and analysis.
- *Methodology notes* (MN) provide a description of what you did and why, your reasons for choosing one approach over another. You can use these notes to keep track of methodological changes you have made and to record the rationale for any such changes.
- *Theoretical notes* (TN) provide the basis for identifying emergent trends and hypotheses. In these notes, you can record changes made to emerging themes and categories, and the reasons those changes were made.

The different categories of notes may be kept separately, of course, but a single file in which they are specified as MN, PN, TN, or FN will also work quite effectively. The different types can be separated and combined with like notes at a later stage.

Data Preparation

As noted above, raw data in qualitative research typically consists of words and images in the form of transcripts or field notes, audio and videotapes, and other paper and computer documents and artifacts. When information and data are received, it is important to organize them so that they can be located when required and stored in the context in which they were collected or observed. In managing qualitative data, therefore, it is important to

- Be systematic and rigorous.
- Record the process you have used in memos, field notes, research logs, or journals.
- Focus on your research questions.
- Aim for an appropriate level of interpretation.
- Recognize the simultaneity of data collection and analysis and the emergent nature of interpretation. (Miles & Huberman, 1994)

Data Analysis

Typically, qualitative data analysis is a combination of both coding down (deduction) and coding up (induction) (Berg, 2001). Induction implies that all themes are emergent from the data; deduction implies that all themes are predetermined. Notwithstanding these differences, to be able to identify themes, patterns, and categories and to record memos and assign codes, there is no substitute for immersion in the data (Abrahamson, 1983; Boulton & Hammersley, 1996; Hammersley & Atkinson 1995; Miles & Huberman, 1994; Patton, 2002; Streubert & Carpenter, 1995).

Typical activities in qualitative analysis are these:

- Coding field notes.
- Making notes in the margins.
- Scanning the materials to identify similar phrases, themes/categories, relationships between them, differences between themes, and differences between groups.
- Isolating these patterns and using them in the next wave of data collection.
- Elaborating themes that cover the consistencies discerned in the data base.

Clearly, these activities result in the generation of copious amounts of information. Computer programs may help organize and manage the information collected during a qualitative study, although methods for data management include pen-and-paper methods as well as computerized systems (e.g., NUD*IST, Ethnograph, NVivo, winMAX, and ATLAS/ti). Both pen-and-paper and computer-based methods often involve developing

- Individual summaries for each case
- Categoric summaries, in which cases are summarized under thematic headings
- Matrix methods, in which individual cases are summarized thematically
- Cognitive mapping, in which maps are developed showing linkages within the data

Although computer-based methods for qualitative data analysis may vary in terms of how data are entered, stored, coded, linked, retrieved, and displayed as well as in their mechanisms for tracking and recording the analytic method (Fielding & Lee, 1998), all of them are capable of performing the kinds of analysis described above.

Pen-and-paper and computerized approaches each have their advantages and disadvantages (see Padgett, 1998). Pen and paper, for example, tends to keep the researcher closer to and more immersed in the raw data for longer. This is both an advantage and a disadvantage; time spent with the data is invaluable, but time is a vital resource when working with a deadline. Computer programs are typically faster and more efficient at sorting and retrieving data but with the commensurate potential that the researcher using them will have less familiarity with the source data and may fail to identify important connections. Neither method is inherently superior, however. What is more important is that you pay attention to ensuring that the approach you select is consistent with your objectives and will help you in the later stage of interpretation.

Whichever method or combination of methods you choose it should

- Allow you to remain grounded in the data.
- Let analytical ideas and concepts emerge.

- Preserve the link between raw and summarized data.
- Permit inter- and intracase search and retrieval.
- Foster transparency so that you are able to describe exactly what you did. (Padgett, 1998; Spencer, Ritchie, Lewis, & Dillon, 2003)

The central component of data analysis in qualitative research is the search for themes in the data. Themes are those unifying ideas that are recurrent elements in the data, and a large part of the skill of qualitative data analysis is in identifying and sorting them. The sources of these themes are often a mystery to novice qualitative researchers. Fortunately, several reciprocal sources of theme development have been discussed in the literature (Bulmer, 1979; Maxwell, 1996; Strauss, 1987). Though the primary source of themes is the textual data itself, other sources include the literature, preexisting professional definitions, commonsense constructs developed by the participants or the researcher, theoretical orientation, values, and structuring of the research question. The search for themes is a function of the qualitative method being used; grounded theory, for example, uses various types of coding (Padgett, 1998).

- *Open coding.* In grounded theory, generative or open coding is the process of theme identification and category development. It is an open process because the researcher approaches the data with no prior assumptions about what might emerge. (Strauss, 1987)
- *Axial coding,* another term generally used in the context of grounded theory, is the process of building connections within and between categories and subcategories.
- *Selective coding* reflects the structural relationship between categories, core categories, and related categories, which are integrated to form the theoretical structure of the analysis.
- *Factual coding,* or descriptive coding, records tangible aspects such as actions, definitions, events, people, places, properties, conditions, and so on.
- *Interpretive coding* records more abstract aspects, such as feelings, thoughts, causal conditions, perspectives, and others.

What is often difficult to find is guidance on how to go about systematically identifying themes. Ryan and Bernard (2003) provide very helpful guidance describing 12 different methods for discovering themes in texts; these fall into four broad categories:

- Word analysis
- Careful reading
- Linguistic features
- Physical manipulation of texts

The 12 methods explicated by Ryan and Bernard (2003) are described below.

Word repetition. This method is based on the notion that to discover what people are talking about, it is helpful to look at the words they use. Techniques include identifying word repetition, looking for key indigenous terms, and finding key words in context.

Indigenous categories. These are in contrast to researcher-defined categories; here you would look for unfamiliar phrases or familiar phrases used in unfamiliar ways. This technique is very similar to in-vivo coding in grounded theory (Strauss 1987; Strauss & Corbin 1990).

Key words in context (KWIC). Despite the acronym, this is a time-consuming though we believe important method of data analysis, since it demands close scrutiny of the textual data. The technique requires that you search for all instances of a particular word or phrase and copy it and the textual context in which it occurs. A simple word processing search or "find" function will help with this task. When you have identified the key words, then you can sort the examples into those with similar meanings.

Compare and contrast or constant comparison (Glaser, 1978; Glaser & Strauss, 1967; Strauss & Corbin, 1990). This is a line-by-line analysis of text in which you might ask,"What is this about?" "How does it compare to the statements before/after?" You might also ask hypothetical questions like "What if this answer had been from a man instead of a woman?" or "What does this remind me of?" (Ryan & Bernard, 2003).

Social science queries, or perhaps for our purposes, social work queries. These involve the search for textual data that will shed light on questions that are important to social work, social science, or your particular research question, in contrast to seeking participant themes (Spradley, 1980).

Searching for missing information. This is the opposite of many other methods of theme identification. Instead of identifying themes that emerge from the text, you can engage in the search for themes that are missing in the text. What is not mentioned? What is the metaphorical elephant in the room? Absence of a theme may represent an issue that people are unwilling to discuss, or at least to discuss in the presence of a researcher. On the other hand, a missing theme may represent assumptions made by participants that you share their assumptions, worldview, or understanding and therefore they do not need to "state the obvious."

Metaphors and analogies. This technique is based on the observation that people often use analogies, metaphors, and similes to represent what they think and how they act (Lakoff & Johnson, 1980). In this technique, you would look for metaphors and then attempt to determine the underlying principles that might represent patterns or themes.

Transitions. The examination of transitions involves seeking the movements that occur between paragraphs in written data, between speakers in oral-based data, or within speeches when one person is speaking.

Connectors. This technique involves examination of words or phrases that imply

Causal relationships, e.g., *because, since, as a result*
Conditional relationships, e.g., *if, then, rather than, instead of, in contrast*
Taxonomies, e.g., *lists, groups, and categories*
Time-oriented relationships, e.g., *before, after, then,* and *next*
Negative characteristics, e.g., *not, no, none,* or the prefix *non*

Unmarked texts. This technique involves examining those parts of your textual database that have not been associated with a theme. By continually reading the text multiple times, it is possible to identify important themes that you can highlight with different colors. Focusing on the unmarked text with each subsequent read may reveal new or less obvious themes.

Pawing. Just what it sounds like; constantly examining each page of the text and marking it with highlighters or colored pencils.

Cutting and sorting. Also just what it sounds like; cutting quotes from copies of the textual database and sorting them into piles that appear to go together (Ryan & Bernard 2003). Of course, the cut-and-paste functions of word processing packages have largely taken over this role.

Many of these techniques overlap or are reciprocal—for example, pawing the data and looking for unmarked texts are the mechanisms by which you may identify word repetition, indigenous categories, and key words in context.

In summary, developing a data management plan before you embark upon data collection is important whether your study is qualitative or quantitative. A sound data management plan will ensure the protection of data confidentiality, fidelity, and integrity. As with all other steps in the research process, data management should be consistent with the research paradigm in which you are operating and should lead naturally to data analysis and eventual structuring of your results.

ACTION STEPS CHECKLIST

- ☐ Develop your data management plan.
- ☐ Determine how you will deal with missing data.
- ☐ Develop a plan for an audit trail.
- ☐ Develop plan for data analysis.
- ☐ Ensure that data management and data analysis are congruent with your method of inquiry.
- ☐ Review, select, and familiarize yourself with computerized data management and analysis software.

7

Writing and Presenting Results

T he satirical news source *The Onion* once ran a spoof story about a welder who was unable to weld because he was suffering from "welder's block" ("Local welder," March 1, 2000). The condition left him staring unproductively at the blank metal for long periods. Many doctoral students reach the final stages of the dissertation experiencing a high degree of lethargy, and some, like the apocryphal welder, struggle with the writer's version of welder's block. Although the process of writing can, and we believe should, be at least moderately taxing, with planning and the adoption of effective strategies it does not have to be excruciating. Therefore, we will discuss strategies to overcome many of the obstacles and issues that make the process of writing seem harder than it should be.

OBJECTIVES

By the end of this chapter you will be able to

- Evaluate your writing habits,
- Identify and rectify those that hinder progress on your dissertation.
- Determine how to organize and present your results.

TOPICS

- You as a writer
- Why writing seems difficult
- Structure
- Content
- Sequence
- Tone and style
- Meaning
- Proofreading and editing
- Data presentation

  o Quantitative
  o Qualitative

- Self evaluation checklist

In Figure 7.1 we have provided a diagram of the dissertation writing process that highlights major questions: What do you want to say (content)? When and where do you want to say it (structure and sequence)? How do you want to say it (tone)? Why is this important (meaning)? Figure 7.1 is also numbered in the order in which writing a dissertation can be approached.

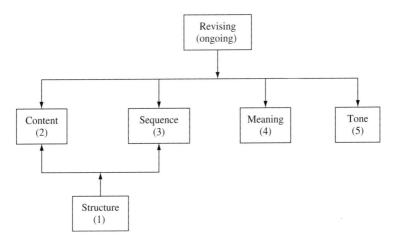

Figure 7.1 Dissertation order

In the interests of space, proofreading, rewriting, and editing are subsumed under "revision" in Figure 7.1; however, all three—proofreading, rewriting, and editing—are continuous processes that occur during and after each of the other stages. The stages are largely but not exclusively linear. Writing one section may require amendments to another, for example. Before moving on to further discussion of structure, content, sequence, tone, and meaning, it is important to give some consideration to you as a writer.

YOU AS A WRITER

The following checklist will help identify your writing habits and where you may be able to make changes to facilitate writing for your dissertation and for the rest of your career. Remember that writing may be one of the largest components of your future career. In a faculty position, you may write for publication, but in many other positions occupied by PhD holders there is an expectation of high-quality, high-quantity written material. The dissertation is likely to be a unique writing experience. Dissertations are intended to be substantial and original pieces of work. Consequently, they are typically longer than any other writing that you will undertake—unless you move on to write book-length documents. Your dissertation is likely to receive more close criticism and scrutiny (from your chair and committee) than any other piece of work that you produce. Peer-reviewed articles do not receive the level of scrutiny typically provided by a dissertation committee.

CHECKLIST 7.1. YOU AS A WRITER

- ☐ Does writing come easily, or is it a challenge for you?
- ☐ What time of the day are you most productive/creative?
- ☐ Do you wait for "divine inspiration" or do you push forward on both good writing days and bad?
- ☐ Do you tend to write everything that comes to mind in long narrative prose and edit later or do you think twice (three times) and craft sentences parsimoniously?

☐ Do you feel guilty when you are not writing?

☐ Do you feel as if you are not writing enough?

☐ Are you worried about what people may think of your writing?

☐ Do you set daily, weekly, any writing goals?

☐ Do you have difficulty starting or do you write the first thing that comes to mind?

☐ Do you have difficulty finishing or can you stop in the middle and pick it up tomorrow?

☐ Do you have a space dedicated to writing or do you write wherever your laptop happens to be?

☐ Do you have a timeline for writing your dissertation?

☐ Do you have time dedicated to writing or do you write between other activities (child care, job responsibilities, etc.)?

☐ Is writing part of your daily/weekly routine?

☐ Do you experience interruptions?

☐ Are interruptions a problem for you?

☐ What are the primary sources of these interruptions?

☐ After an interruption, what do you do?

☐ Are you one of the primary sources of your interruptions?

☐ When writing, do you suddenly notice that your office/house/apartment needs cleaning?

☐ Do you have somebody who can proofread your work?

☐ Do you find it hard to receive and respond to feedback?

As you answer these questions, think about who you are as a writer. The point is that no two people have the same writing style. Ask yourself, will my answers likely contribute to dissertation completion or not? If not, what do I need to change? Know who you are and maximize your strengths. A former teacher of one of the authors, an excellent scholar, researcher, and a terrific writer, once stated that she did her best writing while relaxing on her bed. When her surprised students asked whether she fell asleep, her response was that she did, and when she woke up she would continue writing. We wouldn't recommend this approach for everyone, but it clearly worked in this case.

In the rest of this chapter we will discuss strategies to deal with unhelpful habits. Remember, it is only unhelpful if it inhibits your writing. Feeling guilty about not writing enough may help or hinder, depending upon whether the guilt is debilitating or motivating. To paraphrase Voltaire, perfect is the enemy of good. Instead of striving for perfection with your first draft, aim for "better" with each rewrite. Make each draft the best you can at the time, then rewrite and edit again, and again. Of course, some people may produce a perfect dissertation with their first draft. This particular book is written for the rest of us.

If you have no space dedicated to writing, ask yourself if this lack of space is working for you. Lack of a dedicated space is a problem for many, not just possessing a dedicated space, but the consequences of this lack (interruptions, moving, misplaced material). People generally function more effectively in their writing when they have a private space that is relatively free from interruptions. A cafeteria or coffee shop may have worked for J. K. Rowling and may provide a change of scene to do some of your work, but a dedicated space that allows you to focus and reduces the tendency to engage in task avoidance behavior is enormously helpful. Lack of space is not necessarily a dissertation killer; it may just make a challenging task more difficult.

If you answered no to the checklist questions about having regularly scheduled time to write, or setting goals, or having a long-term plan, think about how to structure your schedule to allow blocks of time dedicated to writing. You may prefer a flexible schedule in which you go through your calendar and mark out the times that you will spend writing, or a less flexible schedule in which you dedicate specific periods of time each day (mornings from 7:00 till 10:00, for example). You may opt for writing for a specified period, or set specific goals, or target a number of pages of output. Whatever system works for you is the system you should choose. Given the significance of writing for your dissertation and the likely significance of writing for the rest of your professional career, it is important to incorporate writing as part of your regular schedule. Working regularly on your dissertation helps to keep the project fresh in your mind and may help offset the vagaries of Hofstadter's Law: "It always takes longer than you expect, even when you take Hofstadter's Law into account" (1999, p. 152). Although self-referencing and whimsical, this is a comment on the difficulty of estimating how long it may take to complete a complex task. A dissertation is a complex task and it may be difficult to predict how long it will take, but the difference between completing and not completing a dissertation is often the difference between having a planned writing schedule and not having one (Acker, Hill, & Black, 1994; Eggleston & Delamont, 1983; Wright and Lodwick, 1989).

Understanding that completion of a PhD requires about 5 years of your life from entry to graduation, the earlier in the process that you adopt a personal schedule or plan, the better. Your school already has a broad plan of study described in the catalogue or program outline, but we are suggesting a much more personal schedule tailored to your dissertation. There is support in the literature for the positive contribution of a structured approach to dissertation completion (Acker et al., 1994), particularly structuring of time (Eggleston & Delamont, 1983; Wright & Lodwick, 1989). Developing a plan early may mean that you have to amend it later, but remember how in clinical supervision it is better to have regularly scheduled appointments that you can change if required rather than to schedule on an ad hoc basis.

In Chapter 2 we suggested developing a proposed dissertation schedule to use in discussion with potential committee members. It might also be helpful to consult one of the many widely available time management books (e.g., Allen, 2001; Fiore, 2006; Forster, 2006; Lakein, 1973; Le Blanc, 2008: Morgenstern, 2004). At the end of 5 years (give or take) of coursework, exams, and writing, you will want to have completed your PhD. What needs to have been completed by the end of year four, year three, year two, and this year to ensure timely completion? To have accomplished the tasks scheduled for the end of year one, what needs to be accomplished by the end of the next 6 months, 3 months, 1 month? Develop goals for each year and for each month within each year, and write them down. To have achieved this month's goals, what do you have to do this week, today, now? (We hope that one of your goals is reading this book.) In resolving what needs to be completed now, it helps to make a "to do" list every day, electronically, on paper, on the Web, or with any mechanism that works for you. When you draw up your daily list make sure you include time spent thinking and planning.

As we said in Chapter 2, each university department has its own culture, style, and philosophy about working together, as does each supervisor. You may work closely with your supervisor and meet frequently, or you may work with a large measure of independence. You should consult with her and factor her into your schedule and time management plan. Determine early what schedule of meeting, writing, and consulting she recommends. As you do so, remember that frequency of supervisory meetings and collaboration with supervisor are positively associated with time to completion (Seagram et al., 1998).

Setting up goals and deadlines helps to harness another whimsical though useful law, Parkinson's (1958) Law; this is often paraphrased as work expands to fill the time allowed to do it. Breaking each task of writing into manageable chunks and then completing them in specified time frames also helps ameliorate the feeling of being overwhelmed that so often leads to procrastination.

Depending upon your own personal style, preference, and circumstances you may find it helpful to meet regularly in a writing group with other doctoral students (pairs or larger groups). If your supervisor expects you to meet with her infrequently, the opportunity to exchange writing drafts or ideas with other doctoral students may be of tremendous help, for both specific feedback and psychological support (Grover, 2007). Again, you can use a writing group to set deadlines and goals. As well as the intellectual struggle that rightly accompanies dissertation research, there is an emotionally demanding component that makes it difficult to know where and how to begin, and to question if you are doing it "right." Sharing your thoughts and ideas with fellow students is an effective way to counter such doubts.

As well as support, feedback from other students provides practice in giving, receiving, and responding to criticism. A dissertation is paradoxically both an independent and interdependent enterprise. While it is important to be able to work independently, it is also important to be able to ask for help when you need it (Grover, 2007). A writing group or colleague may provide answers to some of your queries without recourse to the expertise of your supervisor or committee. You can save supervisory expertise for the really thorny issues.

WHY DOES WRITING SEEM SO DIFFICULT?

Depending upon your previous experiences, the prospect of writing may provoke a variety of unhelpful internal responses. Like Winston, the protagonist in George Orwell's 1984, you may be paralyzed by fear of the consequences of writing. Unlike Winston, whose fear was of the all-pervasive State, however, you may be intimidated by something even more dreadful, your supervisor. You may be apprehensive about writing, knowing that your dissertation advisor's written comments have the capacity to draw blood. You may be struggling with feelings of inadequacy engendered by previous writing experiences, in which the purpose seemed to be that you produced work for it to be eviscerated by somebody's red pen. If not fear or anxiety, then you may be inhibited by the sheer amount of information that you must convey. You may have so many ideas competing to get out of your head that it is difficult to focus on any particular one. Alternatively, you may be bored by the prospect of spending time turning your fascinating research study into something dry, dusty, and academic. These unhelpful habits of thought, allied to other unhelpful habits, may render writing more difficult than it need be.

If you do suffer from these or other unhelpful habits, you are not alone. In developing an inventory to identify and measure psychosocial factors related to dissertation completion in education and clinical psychology, Johnson, Green, and Kleuver (2000) identified two broad characteristics that were negatively related to completion: (1) procrastination, which included self-denigration, fear of failure, difficulty in making decisions, a need for structure; and (2) perfectionism, which included perceptions that the dissertation should be significant and the best in the field.

To understand why writing often appears such a daunting task, it may be helpful to look at the relationship between thinking and writing. The easy thing about writing is that it is merely focused thinking. Of course, this is also the hard thing about writing. In a recursive process, by demanding structure and focus, writing helps to structure and focus thinking, and vice versa. The following thought experiment may help clarify how this works.

Imagine you have to ask your advisor for an extension to hand in an important piece of work because a close family member is ill. By the time you have read the preceding sentence, you have imagined what you need to do. The thinking was easy, spontaneous, immediate, and focused in the present. This simple communication task gathers complexity if conveyed in person, on the phone, in an e-mail, or in a letter. In person you can tell your advisor what you need and why. She can ask clarifying questions and you can correct any confusion caused by the way you structured your request. You can convey your sincerity, contrition, and commitment. Your facial expression and body posture can communicate a combination of earnest and sincere concern with an appropriate (though not obsequious) level of respect. Face-to-face contact also means that you can be reassured she understands and is sympathetic. Her message can be supported by nonverbal communication, demonstrating an appropriate (though not imperious) level of concern. In person, you may also start out of sequence and, at the narrowing of your supervisor's brow, hasten to clarify that you really do have your priorities in order.

If you communicate the same request by telephone you have to convey all the information without the benefit of visual feedback. The task becomes a little more difficult and time-consuming, but you have the opportunity to respond to changes in her tone of voice as well as to specific questions. You may again start out of sequence then say, "Sorry I should have mentioned this before, but ... " In the back and forth of conversation you can clarify, go back, respond to questions, and detect nuances of tone. Again, the thinking involved is relatively easy, spontaneous, immediate, and focused in the present.

If you communicate your request by e-mail, you do not have the benefit of facial expression, tone of voice, or any other nonverbal cues. Therefore, a great deal more care is required in deciding what you need to say, how to say it, and the sequence in which it should be said. It now becomes important to anticipate potential questions and provide information to answer them. E-mail does have the benefit of allowing your supervisor to fire back a quick question for clarification and to receive an equally timely response from you.

Now imagine that your supervisor is on a field trip in remote parts accessible only by letter. Time constraints mean that she will not have the opportunity to write back for clarification. You have to get it right the first time. Invoking the universal intellectual standards (Paul & Elder, 2006) you must be clear, accurate, and precise. Your content must be relevant, you must provide sufficient depth and breadth, and your letter must be logical. The logic should extend not only to the content of your letter but also to the ordering or sequencing of the information. The thinking required is now more complex; it takes more time and is no longer spontaneous. You must have the right structure, content, sequence, and tone. You must anticipate questions about your meaning and deal with them beforehand, thus shifting the focus from the present to the future and demanding more abstract thought in the process. Instead of responding to specific questions one at a time, you must now anticipate a broad range of areas needing potential clarification.

It is evident from this simple thought experiment that thinking for writing is more demanding than thinking for speaking, or just plain thinking. What does this increased complexity mean for your dissertation? As with the formal letter, your dissertation requires that you determine what to say, how to say it, and the structure and sequence in which it needs to be said. You must convey all required information and clarify the meaning and significance of what you have said. In addition, you are required to anticipate all potential questions, providing the information in each section that is necessary to understand subsequent sections.

Thus, structure, content, sequence, tone, and meaning are crucial (see Figure 7.1). Note that we make a distinction between structure, the overall shape of a document (chapters, sections subsections) and sequence, the order in which individual packets of information (paragraphs, sentences, phrases) appear in a document. To get all of this right requires continued and continual proofreading, editing, and rewriting. Indeed, most of writing is rewriting.

Structure

By the time you are writing your dissertation you may have spent many hours talking with your supervisor, fellow students, friends, and family about your research. You know your dissertation topic and can think and probably speak about it with great cogency and fluency.

The next step is to get the words on paper. If you answered yes to the question about difficulty starting in the *You as a writer* checklist earlier in this chapter, or you identified with our impotent welder, Orwell's Winston, or just have too many ideas at once, then adopting an organizational scheme for your writing may help move you forward.

One of the advantages of writing a dissertation is that there is an inbuilt organizational scheme, a preexisting outline, that determines the shape of the document. The shape is determined by the headings used for each chapter and subsection within each chapter. A sample structure for a typical five-chapter dissertation is included in Appendix 7A at the end of this chapter. The internal structure arises from the formality of the dissertation requirements as well as from the particular research activities you undertake.

Phillips and Pugh (2005) identify two different types of writer: serialists and holists. The serialists plan their writing in detail before putting pen to paper or finger to keyboard. The holists think as they write and work through a succession of different drafts. We believe that writing without planning is a problematic practice and that most people are somewhere between these two poles. Dissertations require planned writing but carry the advantage that the overall outline is largely predetermined, particularly for quantitative dissertations.

The chapter structure provides the framework to address many of the questions about where specific content should be placed. Start with this structure or one that you think will reflect the shape of your dissertation and build an electronic or paper version of it. As you start working through your literature review, methods, results, and so forth, you can move the information you have into the relevant electronic or paper folder. Literature review material should appear first in the literature review, not in the discussion section. Results should appear in the results section, not in the methodology section. Discussion should be in the discussion section, not in the results section. Material that supports your research but is not crucial to an understanding of it—for example, extensive quotations, photographs, and data collection instruments— should all be placed in appendices. It is surprising how often these seemingly simple decisions go awry and results are revealed in the discussion section or discussions and conclusions occur in the results section. Ask yourself for each packet of information: Where does this belong?

Content

Often it is not the struggle to find something to say that hinders writing but having too many thoughts buzzing around. Starting becomes difficult because writing requires focusing on one item at a time. This problem can be resolved by sequencing material to determine where to start. One simple but effective technique, if you are faced with uncertainty about where to begin, is to make lists of the ideas that you think should be included. You can make the lists in any order and then go through and number them in the order that you believe they should appear.

Another approach is to get the content down first but not necessarily in sequence. The beauty of word processing is the ease of reordering by cutting and pasting. Once you have the content, continuous combing through and reordering the material can be very effective.

If you are having difficulty coming up with lists or you are struggling to order your content, another technique to stimulate thinking is to brainstorm and then record the pattern of your thoughts on paper. Do not try to get ideas down in any linear fashion. Simply write them as key words or phrases anywhere on the page and then link them with lines or arrows where they appear to connect. Start with the word or phrase central to your thoughts and then write down other words or key phrases that seem to be related. Next, go through and number them in what seems like the right order. Turn this into a list and then write a sentence about each keyword and keep adding sentences until you have paragraphs.

As well as lists and brainstorming there is also the brain-dump approach in which you sit, begin writing, and write all the ideas you have in your head about the subject of your focus and then sort them into the correct sequence with judicious cutting and pasting. With the brain-dump approach, the initial writing is important to put your thoughts on "paper." The structure and sequence of the content can be developed later. The common thread with all of these techniques is to get something written; once you have done so, you are writing. When you begin to make changes, you are rewriting—and to reiterate, the art of writing is rewriting.

Many people find it easier to get the words down by starting in the first person and simply describing what they did as if in an e-mail to a friend. Telling the story of what you did may be made easier if you start by writing in the first person. In this phase you are interested in content, not tone or style. To get the content down, it is often easier to relay it as the story of your own actions, particularly with the methods and results chapters. "First I decided what my dependent variables were. I defined them as . . . Then I set up directional hypotheses, which were . . . " The story can continue in this fashion right through to the end of the results section because you are relating your actions and their consequences. The discussion section is a little different. Here you are describing the meaning of what you found and how this relates to the findings of others. You can see that the different sections require different approaches to writing, which you then make seamless when you revise and edit, remembering of course to change all first person narrative to third person eventually.

As we hinted in the introduction to this chapter, it is a fallacy to assume that the dissertation is to be written after qualifying exams or their equivalent. There are numerous opportunities to write sections or whole chapters of the dissertation throughout a doctoral program. Many classes at the doctoral level require reviews of the literature, research methodology papers, and so forth. When these papers are written, you can use them in the relevant sections of the dissertation file structure. These prequalifying exam papers represent an opportunity to assemble the skeleton of the dissertation and even put some meat on the bones relatively early in your program. Of course, you should check with your dissertation chair that you do not cross the boundaries into self-plagiarizing. Beginning the dissertation early and sticking with the same topic have been associated with time to completion of the dissertation (Seagram et al., 1998). Planned use of your primary writing tasks is an important component of dissertation work.

Primary writing is the work you do, or have done, in your doctoral program that is required to satisfy class requirements—the literature review you did for an intervention strategies class, the pilot study for research methods that becomes your dissertation proposal, or the research synthesis paper you did as an independent study that forms part of your literature review. Having a broad idea early in the program about the parameters of your future dissertation allows for the selection of topics for class assignment that can then perform double or triple duty. Double duty is when the work completed for these assignments contributes to your dissertation. Triple duty is when you publish from these papers. You may approach your class instructor early and suggest that you would like to write a publishable paper from the class assignment. Most faculty members will be happy to provide advice and guidance (after you have received your grade) to help move your paper to publication. Going on to the job market with some publications in hand will help alleviate the nagging question that search committees have about whether a newly minted PhD can publish and get tenure.

Each of the different phases of the dissertation requires a different approach to writing and emphasizes different questions (see Table 7.1). The literature review focuses on what research has come before, how it

Table 7.1 Sample Questions to Be Answered in Each Chapter of the Dissertation

Chapter	Questions
Introduction	Why is this study important?
Literature Review	Who has found what?
	What does it mean?
	How does it fit?
	Why does it matter?
Methods	What did you do?
	How did you do it?
	Why did you do it that way?
Results	What did you find?
Discussion and Conclusions	What does this mean? Why does it matter?
	Why is your research important? What did you
	learn? What are the implications of your findings?

Source: Adapted from Grover, V. (2001). 10 mistakes doctoral students make in managing their program. *Decision Line*, *32*(2), 10–13.

relates to your research, and why it is important. When writing your methods section you can use much of the material from your dissertation proposal, remembering to change the content from the future to the past tense. The discussion and conclusion require a similar approach to the literature review with synthesis and critical analysis of your own work, addressing how your results fit with previous findings, what the implications are, and why they are significant.

Tone and Style

Fundamental to all sciences, including social science, is the requirement to communicate discoveries and research findings. Writing the dissertation for your PhD provides an opportunity for you to develop and refine your written communication skills because the dissertation demands that you follow the rigorous rules of scientific presentation.

The nature of scientific writing is both formal and academic and thus the tone of a dissertation is both formal and academic. You will be able to get a good grounding in the tone and style required from reading other dissertations and journal articles and consulting the APA manual or equivalent guidelines used by your institution. Remember, you are aiming for consistency of tone throughout the document, except when you are quoting other people. Two important adjectives used to describe a dissertation are "original" and "substantial." The research performed to support a dissertation must be both original and substantial, and the finished product must show it to be so. This does not mean, however, that your writing should be littered with jargon or should be unnecessarily polysyllabic.

You are seeking to satisfy the same universal intellectual standards for your work that you applied to the work of others in reviewing the literature. The first of these is clarity, which can be aided if you read your work aloud to get a sense of its sound—the rhythm, punctuation, sentence length, paragraph structure, and flow. Clarity demands that every sentence in your dissertation must be grammatically correct, unambiguous, and in the right tense. APA style typically demands that papers be written in the past tense ("Tom reported . . . ") or the present perfect ("The work of Gerry has shown . . . ").

You should not use contractions (don't use 'em), colloquialisms, or slang terms (except when quoting speech). Accuracy requires that you make fine distinctions in your dissertation because shades of meaning matter. Your choice of words must convey the precise meaning that you intend and must be relevant to the topic of your sentence and paragraph. You and your reader should be able to follow a logical progression in your argument, with contentions supported by citations or by your original work.

Proofreading, Revising, and Editing

It cannot be stated too often that most of writing is rewriting. You must be able to edit your own work and to seek and respond to appropriate feedback from others. Writing and rewriting may be thought of as both organic and mechanistic processes. Before the advent and widespread use of word processing, most writing was done by hand and then transcribed by typewriter, or less frequently typed directly. The much wider access to keyboard activities now means that most students can type. Word processors will check spelling and grammar as well as allow for cutting and pasting and rearranging sequence and structure. There is still room for the lowly pen and pencil when editing, however. Reading from the screen provides one view of your document; how it looks on paper provides another. Many writers now make use of the mechanistic process of word processing to get a formal shape and look to their work, and then print it off and go over it with a pen. This practice, though

> **I love Paris in the
> the spring.**

Figure 7.2 Word blindness

perhaps more time-consuming, allows the organic process of handwriting to improve the flow of the document and helps you identify typing mistakes and other errors that were obscured with the screen view.

One of the most difficult areas of writing for many students is editing their work. Two of the factors that make editing difficult are word blindness, caused by familiarity with what was intended, and over-attachment disorder. The problem of word blindness is exemplified by Figure 7.2.

When most people first read the phrase in Figure 7.2, they do not realize that the word "the" is repeated; they believe they know how the phrase is supposed to read. When applied to a document the size of a dissertation, the problem of selective visual attention (Desimone & Duncan, 1995) is of a different order of magnitude. You wrote it and you know what you intended to say, which means that you may be blind to small mistakes. The problem of word blindness has a number of partial solutions. First, make sure that you use the spell-check function on your word processor; second, use the grammar checker, or proof-reader; third, read your document out loud; fourth, have somebody else proofread what you have written before it gets to your dissertation advisor. Even though your advisor may identify many blemishes in your dissertation, you should not rely on her for proofreading.

Over-attachment disorder becomes manifest when you have written such beautiful words that you find it almost impossible to part with any of them. After all, they are the progeny of your sweat and tears, conceived by the marriage of late nights and hard work. It is possible to become so attached to a wonderful turn of phrase that it is very difficult to hit the delete key.

Many of the parts in cars appear just as beautiful to the engineers who design them. Despite their functional and relative beauty, you are unlikely to be given an extra catalytic converter or spark plug when you buy a car. Car manufacturers use the exact number of parts required to make vehicles function and no more. Extra parts are confusing and it is difficult to know exactly what to do with them. Some of you may be thinking that as impoverished students, the cars you are driving defeat this argument because they are such lemons. Now, ask yourself if you want your dissertation to be considered a lemon. If the words are superfluous, no matter how nicely they flow, cut them. If they are confusing and it is difficult to know exactly what to do with them, cut them. If it makes it easier, you can keep another word processing file open for the material you cut out. You never know, you may even get enough from the deletions for a publication. Just remember the advice from Strunk and White (1976) to would-be writers:

> A sentence should contain no unnecessary words, a paragraph no unnecessary sentences for the same reason that a drawing should contain no unnecessary lines and a machine no unnecessary parts. (p. 23)

Although many of the writing, revising, proofreading, and editing activities are simultaneous, it is still a helpful practice to engage in specific types of editing. We recommend that you use checklists 3.1, 3.2, and 3.3, presented in Chapter 3 (as aids to evaluating the research of others) to evaluate your own research.

You might also make specific edits such as the line edit in which you go over each line one at a time and check for typing errors, punctuation, varied sentence length, appropriate language, grammar, and syntax. You should also go through and remove all or most adverbs. It is also helpful to check for content, consistency, tone, and style as well as check for any loose ends. Your tasks at the editing stage include ensuring that your dissertation is clear, correct, concise, comprehensible, and consistent. Check for spelling, use of terminology and technical terms, grammatical and semantic errors, and the format of your document (Butcher, Drake, & Leach, 2006).

Another factor to consider throughout your writing and particularly as you edit is to avoid bias in your language. The use of nonbiased language is crucial in a scientific dissertation. The APA manual and many other source books on technical writing provide guidance on how to accomplish this important requirement. Make sure that you are familiar with and use the advice from the APA manual about the use of nonprejudicial language.

Constructions that might imply bias against persons on the basis of gender, sexual orientation, racial or ethnic group, disability, or age should be avoided. Scientific writing should be free of implied or irrelevant evaluation of the group or groups being studied (APA, 2007, p. 61).

In addition, it is important to be sure that text citations are in the reference list in the right order, and that the spelling of author names, and dates are the same in both places.

DATA PRESENTATION: QUANTITATIVE

One of the major requirements of dissertation research is organizing the evidence and associated discussion into a coherent form. One way to approach this requirement in writing the results section is to complete all tables first. Tables encapsulate much of the detail of your findings, and as you describe them they can be used as a framework for the narrative. The results section is often one of the easiest sections to organize in a quantitative dissertation. There is a typical structure that begins with details of the sample, how participants were allocated to different groups or conditions, or if the different groups were naturally occurring. Demographic and other salient features of each group should be reported. The sequence then flows naturally into a restatement of your first hypothesis, the data analysis conducted to test the hypothesis, and then the outcome data that correspond to the test. Drawing up the tables that capture this information may also help jump-start your writing.

When you are reporting statistical data or results of statistical tests, use frequencies for categorical variables and percentages when reporting ordinal variables. Interval and ratio data should be presented with the associated sample size (N), mean (m) and standard deviation (σ). Whenever you report a mean score, make sure that you also include the N and σ, just as when reporting percentages you should also report the sample size. When reporting the results of inferential tests, you must include the name of the test (e.g., t- test) and the associated degrees of freedom, the test coefficient, and the alpha level (e.g., $p = .03$). As we discussed in Chapter 4 it is also important, very effective, and sometimes necessary to include a measure of effect size or proportion of variance explained. It is good practice to include a discussion of the power analysis conducted to set your result in context and to include discussion of any adjustment you did to compensate for multiple comparisons (e.g., Bonferroni or other methods for adjusting the probability level to compensate for multiple comparisons). In addition, it is helpful to include confidence intervals where appropriate and the version of the software used to conduct the data analysis.

Tables, Charts, and Graphs

In developing tables to present your data, remember that their purpose is to provide numerical evidence to support information contained in the text. Tables should therefore present meaningful data that are unambiguous and should do so efficiently (Klass, 2008). Meaningfulness in this context is closely related to the universal intellectual standard of relevance, just as presenting tabular data in an unambiguous fashion is akin to the intellectual standards of clarity, accuracy, and precision. These qualities are evidenced in the titles, data, headings, and notes. The text should define each number in the table with clarity and precision. Without repeating all of the information that is contained in tables, the text associated with each table should convey the relevance and purpose of the table, as well as clarifying all terms and abbreviations (Klass, 2008). Efficient tabular display of information is a measure of the logic used in putting the table together and in the capacity to minimize the ink to data ratio (Tufte, 1983). Tables are most useful when they can convey significant information more efficiently or effectively than narrative. A table is most effective when it conveys information or ideas about the data that would not be so obvious in the narrative. A guide for reporting tabular data is to use a table for six or more data elements. If you have fewer than six elements, these should remain in the narrative. Tables of two or fewer columns or rows are better dealt with as part of the narrative, not in tabular form.

The standards of efficient, meaningful, and unambiguous presentation also apply to figures and charts. In the same way that statistics are used to simplify data by representing a large set of numbers with a much smaller set, charts should simplify numerical comparisons. Table, charts, and figures should all be self-explanatory. One of the most common errors made by students is the provision of incomplete information in table titles, heads, and notes. Just because information in a series of tables can be repetitive is no reason not to include it in every table. If your dissertation will contain a number of figures we suggest you consult further references (e.g., Few, 2004: Klass, 2008; Kosslyn, 1994; Mattaini, 1993: Tufte, 1983; Wainer, 1997) including the APA manual and most important, the guidelines for your institution.

Each table, figure, or chart is typically set on a separate page, but as with all issues of dissertation structure and style it is sensible to check once again the requirements from your institution. The APA style manual is an invaluable resource with a minimalist style for tabular structure and guidelines about tabular display that are helpful even if they are not identical to those of your institution. You should be familiar with APA format in any case, as it is the style manual for publication in most social work journals. Finally, make sure that you refer to each table in the text of the chapter and that you have a consistent numbering sequence that remains in the right order throughout the document.

DATA PRESENTATION: QUALITATIVE

Sorting qualitative data can be compared to the process of sorting several loads of laundry in a house with two parents and several children. The clothes are all jumbled and mixed together in no particular order and may be thrown in a pile. The task is then to comb through and make the major distinctions, allocating towels, sheets, and other shared items to one pile, sorting the rest in piles allocated to specific family members: Mom's, Dad's, and each individual child's. Once these major distinctions are made, the piles can be dealt with as separate more manageable entities. Little Johnny's clothes sorted into shorts, shirts, T-shirts, boxers, socks, sweaters, and so on for each member of the family. This production of order by combing through, sorting, and combining is analogous to the task of bringing order to the chaos of raw qualitative data. Both tasks also involve combing through, sorting, and combining.

Two major departures from the data-as-laundry metaphor arise because there are multiple ways in which data may be compiled, arranged, and presented, and because the use of computers with the appropriate qualitative data analysis software can help structure the process of data analysis. Unfortunately, to the best of our collective knowledge, no such method exists to facilitate the process of laundry sorting (yet)! Chenail (1995) suggested several ways in which qualitative data may be presented. These include

- *Natural,* in which data are presented based upon the phenomenon studied. Observation of professional caregivers in a hospice may follow the flow of patients from diagnosis, through the stages of grief, death, loss, and so on.
- *Increasing complexity,* which involves beginning your data presentation with the most straightforward finding and example and gradually moving through stages of increasing complexity to allow the reader the opportunity to follow the logic of your argument.
- *Researcher-based chronology,* in which data are presented in the chronological order in which they were uncovered, or discovered by the researcher. What was your first major finding or insight? What came next?
- *Conditional matrix coding,* in which a conditional matrix is constructed around a core variable and then is linked using the six C's: causes, contexts, contingencies, consequences, covariances, and conditions (Swanson, 1986). These concepts are then used sequentially to present the data around the core concept (Sandelowski, 1998).
- *Quantitative,* in which data are presented based upon quantitative principles. What was the most frequent occurrence? What was the modal type of occurrence? How did concepts or occurrences cluster together?
- *Theory based,* in which data are presented based upon developing or developed theory about the phenomena presented.
- *Journalistic and dramatic,* which are polar opposites, with journalistic beginning with the least important or significant finding and moving to the most significant and dramatic doing the opposite.

Chenail (1995) also describes but does not recommend the "no particular order order," which as a strategy has no endearing features and should be avoided. Typically, the order of no order presentation errs on the side of "descriptive excess" (Lofland & Lofland, 1995, p. 165), presenting the data in almost raw form without attempting analysis or interpretation.

It has been suggested that in the analysis of textual data there are two broad categories of approach (Ryan & Bernard, 2003). The first of these approaches uses words as the unit of analysis (e.g., key words in context). The second approach uses codes (e.g., grounded theory). Concept mapping may be described as a hybrid approach that focuses on both words and codes as units of analysis (Jackson & Trochim, 2002). Concept mapping may take several different forms, using differing methodologies and producing different types of result.

In one form, concept maps are created in a hierarchical fashion with the broader, more general and inclusive concepts at the top; these are then connected with other subordinate or subsumed concepts (Novak, 1998; Novak & Gowin, 1997). Typically, each idea is contained in a separate oval or box with the links to subsumed terms connected by lines. The lines between the broad inclusive concepts and the subsumed concepts are interpolated by connective phrases (*derives from, leads to, results in, is part of,* etc.).

Carley and Kaufer (1993) describe a statistical variation of this type of concept mapping, and Trochim takes the method a step further (Jackson & Trochim, 2002; Trochim, 1989) using a model that includes structured group activities linked to multivariate statistical analyses. The output of the group is processed statistically, generating maps of interrelated concepts based upon aggregate responses. The resulting maps are essentially thematic clusters.

The Trochim model is designed for data analysis, but concept maps are ubiquitous devices that may be used at multiple points in the research process. They can be used, for example,

- At the outset of research to frame a project
- In data management to reduce qualitative data to manageable proportions
- In data analysis (as in the Trochim variant) to analyze themes and interconnections
- As a graphic representation of findings (Novak, 1998)

The textual data in a qualitative dissertation may, of course, be accompanied by other media: photographs, video, audio, drawings, maps, poems, crafts, and so forth. The basic principles of efficient, meaningful, and unambiguous presentation are equally important with these media as they are with tables in quantitative data.

For readers and writers of quantitative research, there is a predictable sequence in which results and data are presented (Hypothesis 1 stated . . . ; specific analysis was conducted and the results were . . . ; Hypothesis 2 stated . . . , etc.). This predictability may be absent from qualitative research, which is driven more by the choice of narrative, epistemology, findings, and resultant theory. Data presentation in qualitative research can be facilitated both for the writer and the reader by the establishment of a pattern to the sequence of presentation. It is worth noting that this type of pattern also works with quantitative data.

Chenail (1995) suggested the use of a rhythmic pattern similar to the one below:

- Present the first significant finding.
- Present a supportive example from the data.
- Display the first example of this finding (a quote, a drawing, a photograph, a matrix, a table, a figure, a chart, etc).
- Comment on the first example.
- Transition to the second example of this finding.
- Display the second example of this finding (a quote, a drawing, a photograph, a matrix, a table, a figure, a chart, etc).
- Comment on the second example.
- Transition to the third example of this finding.
- Repeat this pattern until the end of the section and repeat the same pattern in the next section.

This type of sequencing allows you to make a first pass at writing your results using a preexisting format. As you continue to rewrite and edit you will be able to blend commentary throughout and elaborate as necessary.

The balancing of description, analysis, and interpretation is a challenge in qualitative research (Lofland & Lofland, 1995). As with all phases of qualitative research, the written presentation must reflect an understanding of the epistemology and purpose—what might be described as aligning epistemology, data, and interpretive style (Padgett, 1998).

A grounded study, for example, might emphasize the theoretical understandings derived from the data, with the data used to support the theory and also used to demonstrate the construction of the theory. In contrast, an ethnographic study may pay more attention to the "spatial and symbolic boundaries in which human events occur" (Sandelowski, 1998, p. 277), stressing interactions more than theoretical developments.

As we stressed in the discussion of the literature review and the methodology chapters, each part of the dissertation should flow from and be congruent with the epistemology that underpins the research. This internal congruence is required of the results section, both in the way the section is structured and in the way the data are presented.

The requirement for congruence also extends to the discussion of your results. As you summarize your findings, this section of the dissertation gives you the opportunity to tie all of the pieces together. From summation, you can move to interpretation of your findings in the context of the previous literature and of your study question or hypotheses. In addition, you have the opportunity in this section to consider the implications of your findings. As you write about what your findings imply, it is important to consider their relevance for

- *Theory.* Are your results congruent with the theory underpinning your study or with other prevailing theories? Are your findings congruent with numerous theories? If so, what does this mean?
- *Further research.* What do your findings imply about the way future research might be conducted in your topic area? How has your research contributed to any ongoing controversies or issues? What do your findings imply about the future directions or current effectiveness of social work research?
- *Social work practice.* What do your findings imply for the way social workers conduct their everyday work activities? What do your findings say about how social workers should engage with or intervene with clients? What do your findings imply about

the future directions or current effectiveness of social work practice?

- *Social programs*: What do your findings imply about the way social programs are organized or delivered? What do your findings imply about the future directions or current effectiveness of social work programs?
- *Social policy*: What do your findings imply about future directions for social policy or interpretations of current social policy? What do your findings imply about the future directions or current effectiveness of social policy?

All of these questions are particularly relevant in the context of inter-disciplinary dissertation research in order that the unique voice and perspective of the social work profession may be heard.

In summary, writing up your dissertation is more accurately characterized as a marathon than a sprint. Consistent application over time leads to a finished product. You will recall that we suggest looking for opportunities from the outset of your doctoral studies to develop chapters, in whole or in part, as you conduct coursework. As with all other aspects of the dissertation process, planning, critical thinking, and management of resources are crucial. Find where, when, and how you write most comfortably and productively, then put yourself in that place and work at it.

ACTION STEPS CHECKLIST

- ☐ Identify your writing habits.
- ☐ Eliminate unhelpful habits.
- ☐ Identify a place to write and the best times to do so.
- ☐ Develop a writing schedule and timeline with targets and goals.
- ☐ Develop the skeletal structure of your dissertation.
- ☐ Check for clear, efficient, meaningful, and unambiguous presentation of all text, tables, charts, and figures.
- ☐ Proofread.
- ☐ Have somebody else proofread.

Appendix 7A

Sample Structure for a Typical Five-Chapter Disseration

Chapter 1. Introduction

Introduction
Background
Statement of the problem
Purpose of the study
Significance
Research question(s)
Hypotheses

Chapter 2. Review of the literature

Introduction
Organization of the literature review
Inclusion and exclusion criteria
Conceptual framework
Theoretical framework
Synthesis of literature
Critical analysis
Conclusions and implications

Chapter 3. Methods

Introduction
Research design
Questions and/or hypotheses
Sample selection
Population and sample
Unit of analysis
Power analysis
Variables
Instrumentation
Pilot
Data collection procedures
Data collection and analysis
Bias and error
Reliability, validity, credibility,
trustworthiness
Summary

Chapter 4. Results

Introduction
Organization of results
Summary of methodology
Sample
Results
Summary of results

Chapter 5. Conclusion and Discussion

Introduction
Summary of results
Discussion of results
Relationship of results to previous
findings
Relationship of results to theory
Implications for further research
Implications for policy and practice
Limitations
Summary and conclusion

References

AASW (Australian Association of Social Workers). (2002). *AASW Code of Ethics* (2nd ed). Canberra: Author.

Abrahamson, M. (1983). *Social research methods.* Englewood Cliffs, NJ: Prentice Hall.

The academic job forum. (2004). *Chronicle of Higher Education, 50*(24), p. A11.

Acker, S., Hill, T., & Black, E. (1994). Thesis supervision in the social sciences: Managed or negotiated? *Higher Education, 28*, 483–498.

Acock, A. C. (1997). Working with missing data. *Family Science Review,* 10, 76–102.

Adams, G. B., & White, J. D. (1994). Dissertation research in public administration and cognate fields: An assessment of methods and quality. *Public Administration Review, 54*(6), 565–576.

Allen, D. (2001). *Getting things done: The art of stress-free productivity.* New York: Viking.

Allison, P. D. (2001). *Missing data.* Thousand Oaks, CA: Sage.

ANZASW (Aotearoa New Zealand Association of Social Workers). (2007). *Code of Ethics.* Christchurch: Author.

American Philosophical Association. (1990). *Critical thinking: A statement of expert consensus for purposes of educational assessment and instruction.* The Delphi Report, Committee on Pre-College Philosophy. (ERIC Document Reproduction Service No. ED 315 423)

Anastas, J. W. (2004). Quality in qualitative evaluation: Issues and possible answers. *Research in Social Work Practice, 14*, 57–65.

Anastas, J. W. (2006). Employment opportunities in social work education: A study of jobs for doctoral graduates. *Journal of Social Work Education, 42*(2). 195–209.

Anastas, J. W. (2007). *The next generation of social work educators now: Findings from a national survey of doctoral students.* Paper presented at the 53rd Annual

Meeting of the Profession, Council on Social Work Education, San Francisco, CA, January 19–23.

Anastas, J. W. (2008). *Preparing doctoral students for research: Students' views from a national survey.* Paper presented at the 11th Annual Meeting of the Society for Social Work and Research, Washington, DC, January 19.

Anastas, J. W. (Chair), Bronson, D. E., Crook, W., Doueck, H. J., Harold, R. D., Ross-Sheriff, F., Tucker, D. J., & Wilson, R. (2003). *Guidelines for quality in social work doctoral programs* (rev.). Retrieved February 18, 2008, from http://web.uconn.edu/gade/gadeguidelines.pdf.

Anderson, L. W., & Krathwohl, D. R. (Eds.). (2001). *A taxonomy for learning, teaching, and assessing: A revision of Bloom's taxonomy of educational objectives.* New York: Longman.

Anonymous. (1999). Danger of over-dependence on peer-reviewed publication. *Nature, 401, 727.*

APA (American Psychological Association). (2007). *Publication manual of the American Psychological Association* (5th ed.). Washington, DC: Author.

Armstrong, S. J., Allison, C. W., & Hayes, J. (2004). The effects of cognitive style on research supervision: A study of student-supervisor dyads in management education. *Academy of Management Learning and Education, 13*(1), 41–64.

Azuma, R. T. (1997) A graduate school survival guide: "So long and thanks for the PhD!" Retrieved September, 27 2007, from http://www.cs.unc.edu/~hitch4.html.

Barker, C., & Pistrang, N. (2005). Quality criteria under methodological pluralism: Implications for conducting and evaluating research. *American Journal of Community Psychology, 35*(3–4), 201–212.

Baron, R., & Kenny, D. (1986). The moderator-mediator variable distinction in social psychological research: Conceptual, strategic, and statistical considerations. *Journal of Personality and Social Psychology, 51,* 1173–1182.

BASW (British Association of Social Workers). (2002). *Code of ethics.* Birmingham, UK: Author.

Bell, H. (2004). Balancing power through community building: Setting the research agenda on violence against women. *Affilia, 19*(4), 404–417.

Berg, L. (2001). *Qualitative research methods for the social sciences* (4th ed.). Needham Heights, MA: Allyn & Bacon.

Berger, A., Kirshstein, R., & Rowe, E. (2001). *Institutional policies and practices: Results from the 1999 National Study of Postsecondary Faculty, Institution Survey,* Table 2.1. Washington, DC: U.S. Department of Education, National Center for Education Statistics (NCES).

Best, J. W. (1970). *Research in education.* Englewood Cliffs, NJ: Prentice Hall.

Bisman, C. (2004). Social work values: The moral core of the profession. *British Journal of Social Work, 34,* 109–123.

Blommaert, J. (2005). *Discourse*. Cambridge, UK: Cambridge University Press.

Bloom, B. S. (1956). *Taxonomy of educational objectives, Handbook 1: The cognitive domain*. New York: David McKay.

Bloom, M., Fischer, J., & Orme, J. (2006). *Evaluating practice: Guidelines for the accountable professional* (5th ed.). Boston: Allyn & Bacon.

Bogdan, R. C., & Biklen, S. K. (1982). *Qualitative research for education: An introduction to theory and methods*. Boston: Allyn & Bacon.

Boulton, D., & Hammersley, M. (1996). Analysis of unstructured data. In R. Sapsford & V. Jupp (Eds.), *Data collection and analysis* (pp. 282–297). London: Sage.

Bourner, T. (1996). The research process: Four steps to success. In T. Greenfield (Ed.), *Research methods: Guidance for postgraduates* (pp. 7–11). London: Arnold.

Bowen, W. G., & Rudenstine, N. L. (1992). *In pursuit of the PhD*. Princeton, NJ: Princeton University Press.

Bryman, A. (2001). *Social research methods*. Oxford, UK: Oxford University Press.

Bryman, A. (2006). Integrating quantitative and qualitative research: How is it done? *Qualitative Research, 6*(1), 97–113.

Bulmer, M. (1979). Concepts in the analysis of qualitative data. *Sociological Review 27*(4), 651–677.

Burnett, P. (1999). The supervision of doctoral dissertations using a collaborative cohort model. *Counselor Education and Supervision, 39*(1), 46–52.

Burtless, G., & Orr, L. L. (1986). Are classical experiments needed for manpower policy? *Journal of Human Resources, 21*(4), 606–639.

Butcher, J., Drake, C., & Leach, M. (2006). *Butcher's copy-editing: The Cambridge handbook for editors, copy-editors and proofreaders* (4th ed.). Cambridge, UK: Cambridge University Press.

Campbell, D. T. (1984). Can we be scientific in applied social science? In R. F. Conner, D. G. Altman, & C. Jackson (Eds.), *Evaluation Studies Review Annual, 9*, 26–48.

Campbell, D. T., & Stanley, J. C. (1963). *Experimental and quasi-experimental designs for research*. Chicago: Rand McNally.

Carley, K., & Kaufer, D. (1993). Semantic connectivity: An approach for analyzing symbols in semantic networks. *Communication Theory, 3*, 183–213.

Carlin, D. B., & Perlmutter, D. (2006). Advising the new adviser. *Chronicle of Higher Education, 53*(3) 66.

Carmines, E. G., & Zeller, R. A. (1991). *Reliability and viability assessment*. Thousand Oaks, CA: Sage.

Carter, R. (1997). *Investigating English discourse*. London: Routledge.

Chambers, E. (2000). Applied ethnography. In N. Denzin & Y. Lincoln (Eds.), *Handbook of qualitative research* (2nd ed., pp. 851–869). Thousand Oaks, CA: Sage.

Chenail, R. J. (1995). Presenting qualitative data. *The Qualitative Report, 2*(3). Available at http://www.nova.edu/ssss/QR/QR3-3/plumb.html.

Clark, R., Harden, S., & Johnson, W. (2000). Mentor relationships in clinical psychology doctoral training: Results of a national survey. *Teaching of Psychology, 27*(4), 262–268.

Clemens, R. T. (1996). *Making hard decisions: An introduction to decision analysis.* Pacific Grove, CA: Brooks/Cole.

COA (Council on Accreditation). (2006). *Accreditation standards* (8th ed). New York: Author.

Cochran, W. G. (1977). *Sampling techniques* (3rd ed.). New York: Wiley.

Cohen, J. (1969). *Statistical power analysis for the behavioral sciences* (2nd ed.). New York: Academic Press.

Cohen, J., Cohen, P., West, S. G., & Aiken, L. S. (2003). *Applied multiple regression/correlation analysis for the behavioral sciences* (3rd ed.). Mahwah, NJ: Lawrence Erlbaum.

Cohen, M. Z., & Omery, A. (1994). Schools of phenomenology: Implications for research. In J. M. Morse (Ed.), *Critical issues in qualitative research methods* (pp. 136–156). Thousand Oaks, CA: Sage.

Coleman, M. (2003). Supervision in clinical social work. *Clinical Social Work. 3*(2), 1–4.

Columbia.University School of Social Work. (2008). Leading the profession. NY: Author. Retrieved December 8, 2008, from http://www.columbia.edu/cu/ssw/ phdprogram/experience/leading_profession.html).

Cook, T. D., & Campbell, D. T. (1979). *Quasi-experimentation: Design and analysis issues for field settings.* Boston: Houghton Mifflin.

Cosgrove, L., & McHugh, M. C. (2000). Speaking for ourselves: Feminist methods and community psychology. *American Journal of Community Psychology, 28*(6), 815–838.

Council of Graduate Schools. (1990). *Research student and supervisor: An approach to good supervisory practice.* Washington, DC: Author.

Conférence Générale des Poids et Mesures (CGPM). (1983). *Resolution 1 of the 17th Conférence Générale des Poids et Mesures: Definition of the metre.* Paris: Author.

Crabtree B. F., & Miller W. L. (1999). *Doing qualitative research* (2nd ed.). Thousand Oaks, CA: Sage.

Creswell, J. W. (1998). *Qualitative inquiry and research design: Choosing among five traditions.* Thousand Oaks, CA: Sage.

CSWE (Council on Social Work Education). (2007). *National statement on research integrity in social work.* Alexandria, VA: Author.

Dalton, R. (2001) Peers under pressure. *Nature, 413,* 102–104.

Datallo, P. (2008). *Determining sample size: Balancing power, precision, and practicality*. New York: Oxford University Press.

Davis, K. (1994). What's in a voice? Methods and metaphors. *Feminism and Psychology, 4,* 353–361.

Denzin, N. K. (1989). *The research act: A theoretical introduction to sociological methods* (3rd ed.). New York: McGraw-Hill.

Desimone, R., & Duncan, J. (1995). Neural mechanisms of selective visual attention. *Annual Review of Neuroscience, 18,* 193–222.

Dillon, M. J., & Malott, R. W. (1981). Supervising master's theses and doctoral dissertations. *Teaching and Psychology, 8*(3), 195–202.

Dinerman, M., Feldman, P., & Ello, L. (1999). Preparing practitioners for the professoriate. *Journal of Teaching in Social Work, 18*(1/2), 23–32.

Donovan, S. (2002, February). Systematic critique—the art of scientific reading. *Biomedical Scientist,* 1–2.

Doueck, H. J., Bronson, D. E., & Levine, M. (1992). Evaluating risk assessment implementation in child protection: Issues for consideration. *Child Abuse and Neglect, 16,* 637–646.

Drisko, J. W. (1997). Strengthening qualitative studies and reports: Standards to promote academic integrity. *Journal of Social Work Education, 33,* 185–197.

Eggleston, J., & Delamont, S. (1983). *Supervision of students for research degrees.* Birmingham, UK: British Education Research Association.

Einstein, A. (1905). Zur Elektrodynamik bewegter Körper (On the electrodynamics of moving bodies). *Annalen der Physik, 17,* 37–65.

Elliott, R., Fischer, C. T., & Rennie, D. L. (1999). Evolving guidelines for publication of qualitative research studies in psychology and related fields. *British Journal of Clinical Psychology, 38,* 215–229.

Ellis, B. G. (2007). *The copy editing and headline handbook.* Cambridge, MA: Perseus.

Ennis, R. (1962). A concept of critical thinking. *Harvard Educational Review, 32,* 83.

Erdem, F., & Ozen, J. (2003). The perceptions of proteges in academic organizations in regard to the functions of monitoring. *Higher Education in Europe, 28*(4), 569–575.

Erdfelder, E., Faul, F., & Buchner, A. (1996). GPOWER: A general power analysis program. *Behavior Research Methods, Instruments, and Computers, 28,* 1–11.

Feld, S. (1988). The academic marketplace in social work. *Journal of Social Work Education, 24,* 201–210.

Few, S. (2004). *Show me the numbers: Designing tables and graphs to enlighten.* Oakland, CA: Analytics Press.

Fielding, N. G., & Lee, R. M. (1998). *Computer analysis and qualitative research.* New technology for social research series. London: Sage.

Fields, C. D. (1998). Making mentorship count: Surviving PhD programs requires someone who is willing to show the way. *Black Issues in Higher Education, 15*(3), 28–30.

Fiore, N. A. (2006). *The now habit: A strategic program for overcoming procrastination and enjoying guilt-free play.* New York: Penguin.

Fischer J., & Corcoran, K. (2007). *Measures for clinical practice: A sourcebook* (4th ed., 2 vols.). New York: Oxford University Press.

Forster, M. (2006). *Do it tomorrow and other secrets of time management.* London: Hodder & Stoughton.

Frankel, R. M., & Devers, K. J. (2000). Study design in qualitative research–1: Developing research questions and assessing resource needs. *Education for Health, 13*(2), 251–261.

Gabennesch, H. (2006). Critical thinking: What is it good for? (In fact what is it?). *The Skeptical Inquirer.* March, 36–41.

GADE. (Group for the Advancement of Doctoral Education). (2008). Retrieved December 1, 2008, from http://www.gadephd.org/.

Gaff, J. G. (2002). The disconnect: Graduate education and faculty realities: A review of recent research. *Changing Course: Preparing Faculty for the Future,* Liberal Education, *8*(3), 6–13.

Gambrill, D. D. (1990). *Critical thinking in clinical practice: Improving the accuracy of judgments and decisions about clients.* San Francisco: Jossey-Bass.

Gambrill, E. (1999). Evidence-based practice: An alternative to authority-based practice. *Families in Society 80,* 341–350.

Galton, F. (1886). Regression towards mediocrity in hereditary stature. *Journal of the Anthropological Institute, 15,* 246–263.

Garcia, M. E., Mallot, R. W., & Brethower, D. (1988). A system of thesis and dissertation supervision: Helping graduate students succeed. *Teaching of Psychology, 7,* 89–92.

Gee, J. P. (2005). *An introduction to discourse analysis: Theory and method.* London: Routledge.

Gibbs, L., & Gambrill, E. D. (1999). *Critical thinking for helping professionals: A skills-based workbook.* New York: Oxford University Press.

Gibbs, L., & Gambrill, E. D. (2009). *Critical thinking for helping professionals: A skills-based workbook* (3rd ed.). New York: Oxford University Press.

Gilgun, J. (1994). Hand into glove: The grounded theory approach and social work practice research. In E. Sherman & W. J. Reid (Eds.), *Qualitative research in social work* (pp. 115–125). New York: Columbia University Press.

Giorgi. A. (1985). *Phenomenology and psychological research.* Pittsburgh: Duquesne University Press.

Glaser, B. G. (1992). *Basics of grounded theory analysis: Emergence vs. forcing.* Mill Valley, CA: Sociology Press.

Glaser, B., & Strauss, A. (1967). *The discovery of grounded theory:* Strategies for qualitative research. Chicago: Aldine de Gruyter.

Glass, G. V. (1976). Primary, secondary, and meta-analysis of research. *Educational Researcher, 5,* 3–8.

Goffman, E. (1959). *The presentation of self in everyday life.* New York: Doubleday.

Goffman E. (1961) *Asylums: Essays on the social situation of mental patients and other inmates.* New York: Doubleday Anchor.

Goffman, E. (1963a). *Behavior in public places: Notes on the social organization of gatherings.* New York: Free Press of Glencoe.

Goffman E. (1963b). *Stigma. Notes on the management of spoiled identity.* Englewood Cliffs, NJ: Prentice Hall.

Gold, R. L. (1969). Roles in sociological field observations. In G. J. McCall & J. L. Simmons (Eds.), *Issues in participant observation.* Reading, MA: Addison-Wesley.

Golde, C. M., & Walker, G. E. (2006). *Envisioning the future of doctoral education: Preparing stewards of the discipline.* San Francisco: Jossey-Bass.

Goldstein, H. (1994). Ethnography, critical inquiry, and social work practice. In E. Sherman & W. J. Reid (Eds.), *Qualitative research in social work* (pp. 42–51). New York: Columbia University Press.

Gomory, T. (2001a). Critical rationalism (Gomory's blurry theory) or positivism (Thyer's theoretical myopia): Which is the prescription for social work research? *Journal of Social Work Education, 37,* 67–79.

Gomory, T. (2001b). A fallibilistic response to Thyer's theory of theory-free empirical research in social work practice. *Journal of Social Work Education, 37,* 26–50.

Granello, D. H. (2001). Promoting cognitive complexity in graduate written work: Using Bloom's Taxonomy as a pedagogical tool to improve literature reviews. *Counselor Education and Supervision, 40,* 292–307.

Greene, J. C., Benjamin, L., & Goodyear, L. (2001). The merits of mixing methods in evaluation. *Evaluation, 7*(1), 25–44.

Grover, V. (2001). 10 mistakes doctoral students make in managing their program. *Decision Line, 32*(2), 10–13.

Grover, V. (2007). Successfully navigating the stages of doctoral study. *International Journal of Doctoral Studies, 2,* 10–20.

Hammersley, M. (1996). The relationship between qualitative and quantitative research: Paradigm loyalty versus methodological eclecticism. In J. T. E. Richardson (Ed.), *Handbook of research in psychology and the social sciences.* Leicester, UK: BPS Books.

Hammersley, M., & Atkinson P. (1995). *Ethnography: Principles in practice.* London: Routledge.

Hare, W. (1998). *Bertrand Russell on critical thinking*. Paper presented at the Twentieth World Congress of Philosophy, Boston, Massachusetts August 10–15, 1998. Accessed June 23, 2008, from http://www.bu.edu/wcp/Papers/Educ/EducHare.html.

Harrison, D. R., Sowers-Hoag, K., & Postley, B. (1989). Faculty hiring in social work: Dilemmas for educators or job candidates? *Journal of Social Work Education, 25,* 117–125.

Hart, C. (1998). *Doing a literature review: Releasing the social science research imagination.* London: Sage.

Hasche, K., L., Perron, B. E., & Proctor, E. K. (2009). Making time for dissertation grants: Strategies for social work students and educators. *Research on Social Work Practice, 19*(3), 340–351.

Hawking, S. (2002). *On the shoulders of giants: The great works of physics and astronomy.* Philadelphia, PA: Running Press.

Health Insurance Portability and Accountability Act of 1996. P. L. 104–191. 110 stat. 1936.

Healy, M., & Perry, C. (2000). Comprehensive criteria to judge validity and reliability of qualitative research within the realism paradigm. *Qualitative Market Research, 3*(3), 118–126.

Hockey, J. (1991). The social science PhD: A literature review. *Studies in Higher Education, 16*(3), 319–332.

Hoepfl, M. C. (1997). Choosing qualitative research: A primer for technology education researchers. *Journal of Technology Education, 9*(1), 47–63.

Hoffer, T. B., Sederstrom, L., Selfa, V., Welch, S., Reyes, K., Webber, S., Brown, S., & Guzman-Barron, I. (2003). *Doctorate recipients from United States universities: Summary report 2002.* Contract report for the National Science Foundation. Chicago, IL: National Opinion Research Center.

Hoffer, T. B., Welch, V., Jr., Webber, K., Williams, K., Lisek, B., Hess, M., Loew, D., & Guzman-Barron, I. (2006). *Doctorate recipients from United States universities: Summary report 2005: SED Survey of earned doctorates.* Contract report for the National Science Foundation. Chicago, IL: National Opinion Research Center.

Hofstadter, D. (1999). *Godel, Escher, Bach: An eternal golden braid* (20th anniversary ed.). New York: Basic Books.

Hollis, F. (1949). *Women in marital conflict: A casework study.* New York: Family Services Association of America.

ICPSR (Inter-university Consortium for Political and Social Research). (2005). *Guide to social science data preparation and archiving: Best practice throughout the data life cycle.* Ann Arbor: University of Michigan.

IFSW (International Federation of Social Workers). (2004). *The ethics of social work: Principles and standards.* Bern: Author.

Jackson, K. M., & Trochim, W. M. (2002). Concept mapping as an alternative approach for the analysis of open-ended survey responses. *Organizational Research Methods, 5*(4), 307–336.

Jacobson, N. S., & Truax, P. (1991). Clinical significance: A statistical approach to defining meaningful change in psychotherapy research. *Journal of Consulting and Clinical Psychology, 59,* 12–19.

Jansson, B. S., & Dodd, S. J. (1998). Developing a social work research agenda on ethics in health care. *Health and Social Work, 23,* 17–23.

Joe, S., & Niedermeier, D. (2006). Preventing suicide: A neglected social work research agenda. *British Journal of Social Work.* Advance Access published online on November 8, 2006, pp. 1–24. Available at doi:10.1093/bjsw/bcl353.

Johnson, B. R. (1997). Examining the validity structure of qualitative research. *Education, 118*(3), 282–292.

Johnson, E. M., Green, K. E., and Kleuver, R. C. (2000). Psychometric characteristics of the revised procrastination inventory. *Research in Higher Education, 41*(2), 267–279.

Jones, J. H. (1981). *Bad blood: The Tuskegee syphilis experiment.* New York: Free Press.

Jones, M. P. (1996). Indicator and stratification methods for missing explanatory variables in multiple linear regression. *Journal of the American Statistical Association, 91,* 222–230.

Kadushin, A. (1992). *Supervision in social work* (3rd ed.). New York: Columbia University Press.

Karger, H. J., & Stoesz, D. (2003). The growth of social work education programs, 1985–1999: Its impact on economic and educational factors related to the profession of social work. *Journal of Social Work Education, 39,* 279–295.

Keeney, R. (1992). *Value-focused thinking.* Cambridge, MA: Harvard University Press.

Kelly, K. (1990). *Hermeneutics and critical theory in ethics and politics.* Cambridge, MA: MIT Press.

Kerlinger, F. N. (1957). The functions of the university professor of education. *School and Society, 85,* 35–37.

Kerlinger, F. N. (1959). Practicality and educational research. *School Review, 67,* 281–292.

Kerlinger, F. N., & Lee, H. (1999). *Foundations of behavioural research: Educational, psychological and sociological enquiry.* London: Thompson.

Kerns, D. L. (1998). Establishing a medical research agenda for child sexual abuse. Historical perspective and executive summary. *Child Abuse and Neglect, 22,* 453–465.

Klass, G. (2008). *Just plain data analysis: Finding, presenting, and interpreting social science data.* Lanham, MD.: Rowman and Littlefield.

Koblinsky, S., Kuvalanka, K., & McClintock-Comeaux, M. (2006). Preparing future faculty and family professionals. *Family Relations, 55*(1), 29–43.

Koppel, J. (2005). Pathologies of accountability: ICCAN and the challenge of "Multiple accountabilities disorder." *Public Administration Review, 65*(1), 94–108.

Kosslyn, S. M. (1994). *Elements of graph design.* New York: W. H. Freeman.

Kramer, B. J., Christ, G. H., Bern-Klug, M., & Francoeur, R. B. (2005). A national agenda for social work research in palliative and end-of-life care. *Journal of Palliative Medicine, 8*(2), 418–431.

Kuhn, T. S. (1961). The function of measurement in modern physical science. *Isis, 52,* 161–193.

Kurfiss, J. G. (1988). *Critical thinking: Theory, research, practice, possibilities.* Washington, DC: ASHE.

Labov, W. (1972). The transformation of experience in narrative syntax. In W. Labov (Ed.), *Language in the inner city: Studies in the Black English vernacular* (pp. 354–396). Philadelphia: University of Pennsylvania Press.

Labov, W. (1982). Speech actions and reactions in personal narrative. In D. Tannen (Ed.), *Analyzing discourse: Text and talk.* Washington, DC: Georgetown University Press.

Laird, J. (1994). "Thick description" revisited: Family therapist as anthropologist-constructivist. In E. Sherman & W. J. Reid (Eds.), *Qualitative research in social work* (pp. 163–174). New York: Columbia University Press.

Lakein, A. (1973). *How to get control of your time and your life.* New York: P. H. Wyden.

Lakoff, G., & Johnson, M. (1980). *Metaphors we live by.* Chicago: University of Chicago Press.

Laot, F. (2000). Doctoral work in the social work field in Europe. *Social Work in Europe, 7*(2), 2–7.

Le Blanc, R. (2008). *Achieving objectives made easy! Practical goal setting tools and proven time management techniques.* Maarheeze: Cranendonck Coaching.

LeCroy, C. W., & Krysik, K. (2007). Understanding and interpreting effect size measures. *Social Work Research, 31*(4), 243–248.

Lennon, T. M. (2001). *Statistics on social work education in the United States: 1999.* Alexandria, VA: Council on Social Work Education.

Lennon, T. M. (2002). *Statistics on social work education in the United States: 2000.* Alexandria, VA: Council on Social Work Education.

Lennon, T. M. (2004). *Statistics on social work education in the United States: 2002.* Alexandria, VA: Council on Social Work Education.

Lennon, T. M. (2005). *Statistics on social work education in the United States: 2003.* Alexandria, VA: Council on Social Work Education.

Liebow, E. (1967). *Tally's Corner, a study of Negro streetcorner men.* Boston: Little, Brown.

Lincoln, Y., & Guba, E. G. (1985). *Naturalistic inquiry.* Beverly Hills, CA: Sage.

Lipsey, M. W., & Wilson, D. B. (1993). The efficacy of psychological, educational, and behavioral treatment: Confirmation from meta-analysis. *American Psychologist, 48,* 1181–1209.

Littell, J. H., Corcoran, P., & Pillai, V. (2008). *Systematic reviews and meta-analysis.* New York: Oxford University Press.

Little, R. J. A., & Rubin, D. B. (1987). *Statistical analysis with missing data.* New York: Wiley.

Little, R. J. A., & Rubin, D. B. (2002). *Statistical analysis with missing data* (2nd ed.). Hoboken, NJ: John Wiley.

Local welder suffers from welder's block. (2000). *The Onion, March 1, 2000* Retrieved May 30, 2008, from http://www.theonion.com/content/index/3607.

Lofland, J., & Lofland, L. H. (1995). *Analyzing social settings: A guide to qualitative observation and analysis* (3rd ed.). Belmont, CA: Wadsworth.

Lovitz, B. E. (2001). *Leaving the ivory tower: The causes and consequences of departure from doctoral study.* Lanham, MD.: Rowman & Littlefield.

Lyons, K. (2002). Researching social work: Doctoral work in the UK. *Social Work Education* 21(3), 337–348.

Lyons, K. (2003). Doctoral studies in social work: Exploring European developments. *Social Work Education, 22*(6), 555–564.

Lyons, K., and Mannion, K. (2003). Social work doctoral studies: Researching research. *British Journal of Social Work, 33,* 1115–1121.

Mattaini, M. A. (1993). *More than a thousand words: Graphics for clinical practice.* Washington, DC: NASW Press.

Maxwell, J. (1996). *Qualitative research design: An interactive approach.* Thousand Oaks, CA: Sage.

McMillen, J. C., Proctor, E. K., Megivern, D., Striley, C. W., Cabassa, L. J., Munson, M. R., & Dickey, B. (2005). Quality of care in the social services: Research agenda and methods. *Social Work Research, 29(3),* 181–191.

Merton, R. K. (1936). Unanticipated consequences of purposive social action. *American Sociological Review, 1,* 894–904.

Miles, M. B., & Huberman, A. M. (1994). *Qualitative data analysis: An expanded sourcebook* (2nd ed.). Thousand Oaks, CA: Sage.

Miller, J. E. (2004). *The Chicago guide to writing about numbers.* Chicago: University of Chicago Press.

Mishler, E. G. (1986). *Research interviewing: Context and narrative.* Cambridge, MA: Harvard University Press.

Monroe, E. (2002). The role of theory in social work research: A further contribution to the debate. *Journal of Social Work Education 38,* 461–470.

Morgan, D. L. (1996). The relationship between qualitative and quantitative research: Paradigm loyalty versus methodological eclecticism. In J. T. E. Richardson (Ed.), *Handbook of research in psychology and the social sciences*. Leicester, UK: BPS Books.

Morgenstern, J. (2004). *Time management from the inside out: The foolproof system for taking control of your schedule—and your life* (2nd ed.). New York: Henry Holt/Owl Books.

Morrison, J. (2002). Developing research questions in medical education: The science and the art. Editorial. *Medical Education, 36*, 596–597.

Morrow-Howell, N., & Burnette, D. (2001). Gerontological social work research: Current status and future directions. *Journal of Gerontotogical Social Work, 36*(3/4), 63–79.

Motulsky, H. (1995). *Intuitive biostatistics.* New York: Oxford University Press.

Murphy, K. R., & Myors, D. (2004). *Statistical power analysis: A simple and general model for traditional and modern hypothesis tests.* Mahwah, NJ: Lawrence Erlbaum.

NAS (National Association of Scholars). (2007). *The scandal of social work education.* Princeton, NJ: Author:

NASW (National Association of Social Workers). (1996). *Code of ethics of the National Association of Social Workers.* Washington, DC: Author.

NASW (National Association of Social Workers). (2003). *NASW standards for social work practice in clinical social work.* Washington, DC: Author.

NASW (National Association of Social Workers). (2008). *Code of ethics of the National Association of Social Workers* (rev.). Washington, DC: Author.

National Commission for the Protection of Human Subjects of Biomedical and Behavioral Research (National Commission). (1978). *Report and recommendations: Institutional review boards.* Washington, DC: U.S. Government Printing Office.

National Commission for the Protection of Human Subjects of Biomedical and Behavioral Research (National Commission). (1979). *The Belmont report: Ethical principles and guidelines for the protection of human subjects of research.* Washington, DC: U.S. Government Printing Office.

Nettles, M. T., & Millett, C. M. (2006). *Three magic letters, Getting to Ph.D.* Baltimore, Maryland: The Johns Hopkins Press.

NIH (National Institutes of Health). (2004). *Guidelines for the conduct of research involving human subjects at the National Institutes of Health.* Washington, DC: U.S. Government Printing Office.

Novak, J. (1998). *Learning, creating, and using knowledge: Concept maps as facilitative tools in schools and corporations.* Mahwah, NJ: Lawrence Erlbaum.

Novak, J., & Gowin, D. B. (1997). *Learning how to learn.* New York: Cambridge University Press.

Nuremberg Code. (1949). *Trials of war criminals before the Nuremberg military tribunals under Control Council Law No. 10*, 2, 181–182. Washington, DC: U.S. Government Printing Office.

Nye, C. (1998a). Power and authority in clinical practice: A discourse analysis approach to narrative process. *Clinical Social Work Journal*, *26*(3), 271–280.

Nye, C. (1998b). Using stories in dynamically oriented clinical social work: A discourse analysis approach. *Journal of Analytic Social Work*, *6*(1), 5–24.

Ogles, B. M., Lambert, M. J., & Masters, K. S. (1996). *Assessing outcome in clinical practice*. Boston: Allyn & Bacon.

Orwell, G. (1949). *Nineteen Eighty-Four*. Harmondsworth, UK: Penguin.

Padgett, D. K. (1998). *Qualitative methods in social work research: Challenges and rewards*. Thousand Oaks, CA: Sage.

Parkinson, C. N. (1958). *Parkinson's Law: The pursuit of progress*. London: John Murray.

Patton, M. Q. (2002). *Qualitative research and evaluation methods* (3rd ed.). Thousand Oaks, CA: Sage.

Paul, R. (1993). *Critical thinking: What every person needs to survive in a rapidly changing world* (3rd ed.). Rohnert Park, CA: Sonoma State University Press.

Paul, R., & Elder, L. (1996). *Universal intellectual standards*. Foundation for Critical Thinking. Retrieved December 8, 2008, from http://www.criticalthinking.org/resources/articles/universal-intellectual-standards.shtml-top.

Paul, R., & Elder, L. (2006). *Critical thinking tools for taking charge of your learning and your life*. Upper Saddle River, NJ: Prentice Hall.

Paul, R., & Elder, L. (2008). The miniature guide to critical thinking: Concepts and tools. Dillon Beach, California: The Foundation for Critical Thinking.

Payne, M. (2005). *Modern social work theory*. Basingstoke, UK: Macmillan Palgrave.

Phillips, E., & Pugh, D. (2005). *How to get a PhD* (4th ed.). Buckingham, UK: Open University Press.

Ponterotto, J. G., & Grieger, I. (1999). Merging qualitative and quantitative perspectives in a research identity. In M. Kopala & L. A. Suzuki (Eds.), *Using qualitative methods in psychology* (pp. 49–61). Thousand Oaks, CA: Sage.

Popper, K. R. (2002). *Conjectures and refutations: The growth of scientific knowledge*. New York: Routledge.

Preacher, K. J., & Hayes, A. F. (2008). Asymptotic and resampling strategies for assessing and comparing indirect effects in multiple mediator models. *Behavior Research Methods, 40*, 879–891.

Preacher, K. J., Rucker, D. D., & Hayes, A. F. (2007). Assessing moderated mediation hypotheses: Strategies, methods, and prescriptions. *Multivariate Behavioral Research, 42*, 185–227.

Ray, S. (2007) Selecting a doctoral dissertation supervisor: Analytical hierarchy approach to the multiple criteria problem. *International Journal of Doctoral Studies, 2*, 23–32.

Reicher, S. (2000). Against methodolatry: Some comments on Elliott, Fischer, and Rennie. *British Journal of Clinical Psychology, 39*, 1–6.

Riecken, H. W., & Boruch, R. (Eds.). (1974). *Social experimentation: A method for planning and evaluating social intervention.* New York: Academic Press.

Reid, W. J., & Smith, A. D. (1989). *Research in social work* (2nd ed.). New York: Columbia University Press.

Richmond, M. E. (1899). *Friendly visiting among the poor: A handbook for charity workers.* New York: McMillan.

Richmond, M. (1917). *Social diagnosis.* New York: Russell Sage Foundation.

Riessman, C. K. (1993). *Narrative analysis.* Qualitative research methods series, No. 30. Newbury Park, CA: Sage.

Robb, M. (2005). A deepening doctoral crisis. *Social Work Today, 5*(4), 13.

Rosnow, R. L., & Rosenthal, R. (1996). Computing contrasts, effect sizes, and counternulls from other people's published data: General procedures for research consumers. *Psychological Methods, 1*, 331–340.

Rossi, P. H., Freeman, H. H., & Lipsey, M. W. (1999). *Evaluation: A systematic approach* (6th ed.). Thousand Oaks, CA: Sage.

Rossman, G. B., & Wilson, B. L. (1994). Numbers and words revisited: Being "shamelessly eclectic." *Quality and Quantity, 28*, 315–327.

Rubin, A., & Babbie, E. (1997). *Research methods for social work* (3rd ed.). Pacific Grove, CA: Brooks/Cole.

Rubin, A., & Babbie, E. (2007). *Essential research methods for social work.* Belmont, CA: Thomson Brooks/Cole.

Rudd, E. (1985). *A new look at postgraduate failure.* Guildford, UK: SRHE.

Ryan, G., & Bernard, H. R. (2003). Techniques to identify themes in qualitative data. *Field Methods, 15*(1) 85–109. A version of this paper is also available at http://www.analytictech.com/mb870/Readings/ryan-bernard_techniques_to_identify_themes_in.htm.

Sandelowski, M. (1998). Writing a good read: Strategies for re-presenting qualitative data. *Research in Nursing and Health, 21*, 375–382.

Schiffrin, D., Tannen, D., & Hamilton, H. E. (Eds.). (2001). *Handbook of discourse analysis.* Oxford, UK: Blackwell.

Schniederjans, M. (2007). A proposed PhD student bill of rights. *International Journal of Doctoral Studies, 2*, 2–8.

Sciarra, D. (1999). The role of the qualitative researcher. In M. Kopala & L. A. Suzuki (Eds.), *Using qualitative methods in psychology* (pp. 37–48). Thousand Oaks, CA: Sage.

Scourfield, J. (2008). Professional doctorate programmes in social work: The current state of provision in the UK. *British Journal of Social Work*. Advance Access published October 28, 2008, pp. 1–16. Available at doi:10.1093/bjsw/ bcn139.

Seagram, B., Gould, J., & Pyke, S. (1998). An investigation of gender and other variables on time to completion of doctoral degrees. *Research in Higher Education*, 39(3), 319–335.

Sedlmeier, P., & Gigerenzer, G. (1989). Do studies of statistical power have an effect on the power of studies? *Psychological Bulletin*, 105, 309–316.

Shadish, W. R., Cook, T. D., & Campbell, D. T. (2002). *Experimental and quasi-experimental research designs for generalized causal inference*. Boston: Houghton Mifflin.

Shafer, J. L., & Graham, J. W. (2002). Missing data: Our view of the state of the art. *Psychological Methods*, 7, 147–177.

Shek, D. T. L., Lee J. H., & Tam, S. Y. (2007). Analyses of postgraduate social work dissertations in Taiwan: Implications for social work research and education. *International Social Work*, 50(6), 821–838.

Shek, D. T. L., Tang. V., & Han, X. Y. (2005). Evaluation of evaluation studies using qualitative research methods in the social work literature (1990–2003): Evidence that constitutes a wake-up call. *Research on Social Work Practice*, 15(3): 180–194.

Sherman, E. (1994). Discourse analysis in the framework of the change process. In E. Sherman, & W. J. Reid (Eds.), *Qualitative research in social work* (pp. 228–241). New York: Columbia University Press.

Sherman, E., & Reid, W. J. (1994). Introduction: Coming of age in social work— the emergence of qualitative research. In E. Sherman & W. J. Reid (Eds.), *Qualitative research in social work* (pp. 1–15). New York: Columbia University Press.

Sherman, S. R. (1994). Commentary: Grounded theory methods—applications and speculations. In E. Sherman & W. J. Reid (Eds.), *Qualitative research in social work*. (152–174). New York: Columbia University Press.

Shulman, L. (1993). *Interactional supervision*. Washington, DC: NASW Press.

Spencer, L., Ritchie, J., Lewis, J., & Dillon, L. (2003). *Quality in qualitative evaluation: A framework for assessing research evidence. A quality framework*. London: Cabinet Office.

Spradley, J. P. (1980). *Participant observation*. New York: Holt, Rinehart, and Winston.

Stenbacka, C. (2001). Qualitative research requires quality concepts of its own. *Management Decision*, 39(7), 551–555.

Stiles, W. B. (1993). Quality control in qualitative research. *Clinical Psychology Review*, 13, 593–618.

Strauss, A. (1987). *Qualitative analysis for social scientists.* Cambridge, UK: Cambridge University Press.

Strauss, A., & Corbin, J. (1990). *Basics of qualitative research: Grounded theory procedures and techniques.* Thousand Oaks, CA: Sage.

Streubert, H. J., & Carpenter, D. R. (1995). *Qualitative research in nursing— advancing the humanistic imperative.* Philadelphia: J. B. Lippincott.

Strunk, W., & White, E. B. (1976). *The elements of style* (3rd ed.). New York: MacMillan.

Swanson, J. M. (1986). Analyzing data for categories and description. In W. C. Chenitz & J. M. Swanson (Eds.), *From practice to grounded theory: Qualitative research in nursing* (pp. 121–132). Reading, MA: Addison-Wesley.

Tashakkori, A., & Teddlie, C. (2003). *Handbook of mixed methods in social and behavioral research.* Thousand Oaks, CA: Sage.

Taylor, S. J., & Bogdan, R. (1998). *Introduction to qualitative research methods: A guidebook and resource.* New York: Wiley.

Thurgood, L., Golladay, M. J., & Hill, S.T. (2006). *U.S. Doctorates in the 20th Century.* Arlington, VA: National Science Foundation.

Thyer, B. A. (2001). What is the role of theory in research on social work practice? *Journal of Social Work Education, 37*(1), 9–25.

Thyer, B. A. (2002). Evidence-based practice and clinical social work. *Evidence-Based Mental Health, 5,* 6–7.

Thyer, B. A. (2008). *Preparing research articles.* New York: Oxford University Press.

Trochim, W. (1989). An introduction to concept mapping for planning and evaluation. *Evaluation and Program Planning, 12,* 1–16.

Trochim, W. M. (2006). *The research methods knowledge base* (2nd ed.). Retrieved February 22, 2008 from http://www.socialresearchmethods.net/kb/destypes.php.

Trochim, W. M., & Land, D. (1982). Designing designs for research. *The Researcher, 1*(1), 1–6.

Tufte, E. (1983). *The visual display of quantitative information.* Cheshire, CN: Graphics Press.

USDHHS (U.S. Department of Health and Human Services). (2003). *National Institutes of Health: Plan for social work research.* Washington, DC: Author.

Van Maanen, J. (1988). *Tales of the field: On writing ethnography.* Chicago: University of Chicago Press.

Van Maanen, J. (Ed.). (1995). *Representation in ethnography.* Thousand Oaks, CA: Sage.

Wainer, H. (1997). *Visual revelations: Graphical tales of fate and deception from Napoleon Bonaparte to Ross Perot.* Mahwah, NJ: Lawrence Erlbaum.

Walker, G. E., Golde, C. M., Jones, L., Bueschel, A. C., & Hutchings, P. (2008). *The formation of scholars: Rethinking doctoral education for the twenty-first century.* San Francisco: Jossey-Bass.

Walker, S., Ouellette, V., & Ridde, V. (2006). How can PhD research contribute to the global health research agenda? *Development in Practice, 16*(6), 617–622.

Wanta, W., Parsons, P., Dunwoody, S., Barton, R., & Barnes, B. (2003). Preparing graduate students to teach: Obligation and practice. *Journalism and Mass Communication Educator, 58*(3), 209–238.

Weindling, P. J. (2004). *Nazi medicine and the Nuremberg Trials: From medical war crimes to informed consent.* New York: Palgrave Macmillan.

Whittemore, R., Case, S. K., & Mandle, C. L. (2001). Validity in qualitative research. *Qualitative Health Research, 11*, 522–537.

Whyte, W. F. (1955). *Street corner society* (2nd ed.). Chicago: University of Chicago Press.

Willig, C. (2001). *Introducing qualitative research in psychology: Adventures in theory and method.* Buckingham, UK: Open University Press.

Wittman, M. (1979). Feast or famine: The future of doctoral education in social work. *Journal of Education for Social Work, 15*(1), 110–115.

Wolcott, H. F. (1994). *Transforming qualitative data: Description, analysis, and interpretation.* Thousand Oaks, CA: Sage.

Wright, J., & Lodwick, R. (1989). The process of the PhD: A study of the first year of doctoral study. *Research Papers in Education, 4*, 22–56.

Wulf, W., Cohen, E., Corwin, W., Jones, A., Levin, R., Pierson, C., & Pollack, F. (1974). Hydra: The kernel of a multiprocessor operating system. *Communications of the ACM, 17*(6): 337– 345.

Yardley, L. (2000). Dilemmas in qualitative health research. *Psychology and Health, 15*, 215–228.

Young, K., Fogarty, M. P., & McRea, S. (1987). *The management of doctoral studies in the social sciences.* London: PSI.

Zastrow, C., & Bremner, J. (2004). Social work education responds to the shortage of persons with both a doctorate and a professional social work degree. *Journal of Social Work Education, 40*, 351–358.

Index

Note: Page numbers followed by *t* and *f* refer to pages containing tables and figures respectively.